The Rhind Lectures in Archaology

SCOTTISH LAND NAMES
THEIR ORIGIN AND MEANING

By
Sir Herbert Maxwell, Bart., M.P.

HERITAGE BOOKS
2008

HERITAGE BOOKS
AN IMPRINT OF HERITAGE BOOKS, INC.

Books, CDs, and more—Worldwide

For our listing of thousands of titles see our website
at
www.HeritageBooks.com

Published 2008 by
HERITAGE BOOKS, INC.
Publishing Division
100 Railroad Ave. #104
Westminster, Maryland 21157

Copyright © 1894 Sir Herbert Maxwell, Bart., M.P.

W. Blackwood &Sons, Edinburgh & London

Other books by the author:
History of Dumfries and Galloway

All rights reserved. No part of this book may be reproduced or transmitted in any form or by any means, electronic or mechanical, including photocopying, recording or by any information storage and retrieval system without written permission from the author, except for the inclusion of brief quotations in a review.

International Standard Book Numbers
Paperbound: 978-0-7884-0887-8
Clothbound: 978-0-7884-7133-9

PREFACE.

THESE lectures are offered as a contribution to a study conducted until lately on lines the reverse of scientific. What the late Dr Reeves and Dr Joyce have done for the place-names of Ireland, Canon Isaac Taylor has done for those of England, and Mr A. W. Moore for those of the Isle of Man, has never been adequately performed for Scotland. It was my original intention to expand these lectures, condensed from material collected during many years, into a tolerably exhaustive treatise on the subject; but I am advised to publish them at once, just as they were delivered; and I am encouraged by the numbers and attention of those who listened to them in the belief that there are plenty of students ready to apply sound principles and cautious analysis to a branch of archæology and philology at present in a very backward state.

I have, it is needless to say, derived much assistance from the writings of the scholars above mentioned, as well as from those of Professors Rhys and W. W. Skeat, and the late Dr Skene. I have also availed myself largely of the volume on Scottish Place-Names lately published by the Rev. J. Johnston, of Falkirk, who has rendered good service to students by the extensive list which he has compiled.

I regret that the pressure of other occupations has not allowed me to supply what undoubtedly ought to have been given—viz., exact reference to authorities quoted, and the different manuscripts from which old spellings have been collected. I can but offer an apology to my readers for this omission, with the assurance that they may rely on the care with which such extracts have been made.

HERBERT MAXWELL.

MONREITH, *January* 1894.

CONTENTS.

LECTURE I.

GENERAL PRINCIPLES.

                                                                                                                  PAGE

Difficulties to be encountered—Every place-name means something—Permanence of place-names—Their origin not usually poetical, but matter-of-fact—Arbitrary orthography—Importance of early spelling—Changes in vowel sound—The significance of stress—Its movement with the qualitative in compounds—Influence of railways on pronunciation—Popular and map-makers' blunders—Exaggeration—Deceptive forms, . . . 1

LECTURE II.

THE LANGUAGES OF SCOTTISH PLACE-NAMES.

Traces of pre-Celtic speech—The Iverian or Silurian race—The Firbolg of the Irish Annalists—The Ernai—The two main branches of Celtic speech—Obsolete words—The operation of *umlaut*—Linguistic change—Effects of aspiration and eclipse—Difference between Gaelic and Welsh—Q Celts and P Celts—Test words—Similarity of Gaelic and Welsh—Ghost-names, . . . 27

LECTURE III.

THE LANGUAGES OF SCOTTISH PLACE-NAMES.

Pictish speech—Conflict of authorities—Place-names in Pictland—Mythical descent of the Picts—Columba's mission to Pictland—Pictish vocables—Polyglot passage in Bede's Chronicle—The place-names of Galloway—Conclusions—Anglo-Saxon speech—The Frisian colonies—Order of generic and specific in Teutonic compounds—Corrupt forms, ... 54

LECTURE IV.

THE LANGUAGES OF SCOTTISH PLACE-NAMES.

Scandinavian or Old Norse and Danish—Obliteration of Celtic speech in the Northern Isles—Mixture of tongues in the Western Isles—Norse names disguised as Gaelic—Aspiration of Gaelic consonants—Confusion on the maps—Gaelic names disguised as Norse—Relative antiquity of certain place-names—Traces of Norse occupation in Scotland—Resemblance between Norse and Saxon speech—Norse test-words—Their distribution—Inferences therefrom—Mixture of languages in Strathclyde—The Gaelic *dal* and Norse *dalr*—Difference in their meaning—Norse and Saxon loan-words in English, . 76

LECTURE V.

THE LESSON OF PLACE-NAMES.

Succession of races not explained by place-names—These illustrate former appearance of the country—The old forest—Its trees and undergrowth—Humbler vegetation—Crops—Animals locally or generally extinct—The chase—Deer and other animals—Names of animals borne by men, ... 103

Contents.

LECTURE VI.

THE LESSON OF PLACE-NAMES.

The land—Its surface and divisions—Open land inseparable from the idea of fighting—Norse pennylands—Occupations and trades—Crime and punishment—Poverty—Disease—Rivers and streams—Ecclesiastical names—Early dedications of chapels and wells—Priests and monks—Land not usually named by the early Celts from ownership—But frequently so by Teutonic people—Land-names given to men—Men's names given to lands—Conclusion, ... 130

INDEX OF PLACE-NAMES REFERRED TO IN THE TEXT, . . 183

SCOTTISH LAND-NAMES

SCOTTISH LAND-NAMES.

LECTURE I.

GENERAL PRINCIPLES.

DIFFICULTIES TO BE ENCOUNTERED—EVERY PLACE-NAME MEANS SOMETHING—PERMANENCE OF PLACE-NAMES—THEIR ORIGIN NOT USUALLY POETICAL, BUT MATTER-OF-FACT—ARBITRARY ORTHOGRAPHY—IMPORTANCE OF EARLY SPELLING—CHANGES IN VOWEL SOUND—THE SIGNIFICANCE OF STRESS—ITS MOVEMENT WITH THE QUALITATIVE IN COMPOUNDS—INFLUENCE OF RAILWAYS ON PRONUNCIATION—POPULAR AND MAP-MAKERS' BLUNDERS—EXAGGERATION—DECEPTIVE FORMS.

INQUIRY into the origin and meaning of Scottish place-names is a task beset with difficulties of a peculiar kind. Most of these names were conferred by people speaking a language which has long ceased to be heard in the districts where the names remain — a language, moreover, which was practically unwritten, for, unlike Ireland, Scotland possesses but a few uncertain fragments of

Difficulties to be encountered.

Gaelic or Erse literature. Scottish Gaelic, therefore, has never, until recently, been subject to that check which writing and printing set upon the tendency of speech to alter in meaning and pronunciation with every succeeding generation. Even when a language has become thoroughly literary, the process of change, though greatly retarded, still goes on. In English, for example, the changing shades of meaning in popular intensives, such as "awful," "blooming," "tremendous," &c., occurring in ephemeral songs and other light literature, may prove a snare to the student who, in after-ages, shall attempt to interpret them according to their strict etymology.

Every place-name means something.

But there is one sure source of encouragement towards the solution of place-names, in that every such name has a real meaning, however darkly it may have been obscured by linguistic change or phonetic expression in the lips of people speaking another language. No man ever attempted successfully to invent an arbitrary combination of sound-signs to designate a locality: every place-name, in whatever language, is a business-like definition derived from some peculiarity or leading feature, as we might say the Green Hill, the White House, the Oak-wood; or from some incident, as the Battle-Field, the Murder-Stone, the Forge-Hill; or of possession, as John's town, William's field, the Priest's land.

Once localities are thus distinguished, it is very

General Principles.

difficult to dispossess them of the names they have acquired, even though Greenhill should lose all its verdure, though the Whitehouse (or Whithorn—Anglo-Saxon *hwit œrn*) should be pulled down and a red one built in its place, and the oak-wood be levelled with the ground. In A.D. 43 the Roman general Aulus Plautius, in the course of operations against the British King Cunobeline, intrenched himself on the marshy ground above the junction of the Lea with the Thames. There is no record of a town there previous to this, and the Celtic natives probably called it *lon dyn* ro *dún*—London—the marsh fort, to distinguish it, perhaps, from *hen dún*—Hendon—the old fort, the stronghold of Cunobeline, a few miles to the north-west. The place where the Tower of London now stands was then marsh land, and this is a good example of an ancient name preserving a picture of a landscape which has undergone complete change in the process of civilisation. The Roman conquerors altered *lon dún* into Londinium; but in order to commemorate their conquest of Britain, they subsequently decreed that the town which grew up round the camp of Aulus Plautius should be known as *Augusta*, and that, or *Londinium Augusta*, was for a time its official title: yet the simple native name could not be got rid of, and by that name it will continue to be known as long as one of its stones remains upon another.

Now, the lesson of this example is that poetical and metaphorical interpretations of place-names

Permanence of place-names.

should generally be looked on with great suspicion: the true origin is commonly matter of fact.

There is, indeed, a certain class of names of a somewhat figurative derivation, as when we speak of the brow, flank, or shoulder of a hill, from analogy with the human figure. Gùllane, in East Lothian, so well known to golfers, is the Gaelic *guallan*, a shoulder, descriptive of the side of a headland; and the Braid Hills, near Edinburgh, are named from *braghad* (braad), the breast, in the sense of upland. The Norsemen, who have left a deep impression on Scottish topography, call a small island beside a big one a calf, as *Manarkalfr*, still known to us as the Calf of Man, and to the Highlanders as *an Calbh Manannach;* but the motive in such cases is not poetical or sentimental, but an attempt by means of comparison with familiar objects to convey a definition.

Place-names, then, are applied by the automatic operation of the mind, and not by a conscious effort, like that involved in choosing the name for a child or for a villa in the suburbs. The endeavour to trace their significance, though it must often prove unsuccessful, is the pursuit, not of a chimerical hypothesis, like the philosopher's stone, but of an actual, though more or less obscure, entity. The meaning is always there, if we can arrive at it.

<small>Letters only symbols.</small>   The place-names of this country have nearly all been transferred to writing: it must, therefore, be borne in mind that letters—alphabetical characters —are not visible speech; that spelling is but the

mechanical means of representing vocal sounds by a series of symbols which have been agreed on, but have no more organic connection with sound than numerical characters have to number. These symbols, properly treated, are invaluable servants, but, unless kept in their proper place, they become tyrannical masters.

Exactness in spelling is a modern refinement; nothing is commoner than to find a single name spelt in half-a-dozen different ways in the same manuscript. The object of early writers was to give an idea of the sound of a name by employing written characters, and so long as the idea was conveyed, neither writers nor readers troubled themselves about the niceties of orthography. Here, for instance, are five-and-twenty variations in the spelling of the name of my native province, Galloway, collected from official records and other sources:—

Galewalia.	Galwychya.
Galeweia.	Gallua.
Gallewathia.	Galwodia.
Galewia.	Galwallia.
Galleweie.	Galluway.
Galwethia	Galway.
Galwayth.	Gallowaie.
Gallwadia.	Galovidia.
Galwadensis provincia.	Gallovidia.
Galwithia.	Galwela.
Galvidia.	Galloway.
Galuveia.	Wallowithia.
Gallwa.	

All these renderings pretty well conceal the original name, whether that was, as the late Mr Skene taught us, *Gallgaedhel* in Gaelic and *Galwyddel* in Welsh, meaning the land of the stranger Gaels—*i.e.*, the Gaels who served under the pirate kings of Norway and Denmark—or as Professor Rhys, with less probability, suggests, that the Latin form *Galweidia* indicates the name of *Fidach*, in Welsh *Goddeu*, one of the seven sons of Cruithne, the legendary eponymus of the Picts.

<small>Importance of early spellings.</small>

Notwithstanding the uncertainty and confusion of primitive spelling, it is of the first importance to obtain the earliest combination of letters by which a name was represented. When the familiar name of Tweed is found to be spelt *Tuid* in Bede's History and *Tede* in the Pictish Chronicle and in a manuscript of the twelfth century, it becomes easy to recognise it as the same name as *Teith,* a river in Perthshire, anciently written *Teth,* and now called *Thaich* by the Highlanders. It is true that we are still uncertain as to the true meaning, but we are so far on the road to it, inasmuch as the connection has been established between a group of river-names— Tweed, Teith, Tay, Taw, Teviot, Teifi.

Names often lose the character of their original language by being written in another language. There are two places called Leadburn — one in Lanarkshire, among the Leadhills, the meaning of which is pretty obvious; the other in Mid-Lothian, where there is no lead. Who would suspect that the latter was a Gaelic name, unless he knew that it had been written Lecbernard in a charter by which William the Lion (1167-70) conveyed it to Galfrid de Malauilla (Melville)? Here the early spelling shows that the original meaning was *leac Bernard*, Bernard's stone (or grave), or perhaps *leac Birinn*, the stone of St Birrin, from whom Kilbìrnie parish, in Ayrshire, derives its name.

From a charter of the same king it is evident that Granton, near Edinburgh, is not, as it appears, Grant's town, like Grantown-on-Spey; for it is written *Grendun*—the Anglo-Saxon *gréne dún*, green hill. The earliest mention of Grant as a Scottish surname does not occur till nearly one hundred years later than this charter, when, in A.D. 1250, Gregory le Grant appears in history.[1]

Having ascertained the earliest written form of any name, account must next be taken of the changes in English vowel pronunciation which have taken place since this attempt at phonetic writing was made. Let us consider the form given to the well-known name Glenàlmond. It is composed of two Gaelic, possibly Pictish, words, *gleann amuin*, meaning the glen of the river, but the *a* in *amuin* was not sounded as we sound it in "tan," still less like that in "tame," but rather like that in "tar." For

Changes in vowel sound.

---

[1] It is true that an attempt was once made to establish the higher antiquity of this surname by reading the verse in Genesis, "there were *giants* in those days"—"there were *Grants* in those days"!

several centuries the English *a* was pronounced broad, at least in Northern English, and "amon" represented the Gaelic pronunciation closely enough; but when, towards the fifteenth century, *a* (broad) began to be narrowed into *á* (narrow), it became necessary to insert a mute consonant to represent the broad sound. Thus the *amuin* of Mid-Lothian was written Awmon, and the *amuin* of Perthshire was written Almond (a final *d* being added by false analogy with the name of the fruit). Both these rivers are now called Almond; but it is an instance of caprice in spelling that Cràmond on the Mid-Lothian stream— *i.e.*, *cathair amuin*, the fort on the river—has not received the redundant *l*, so you shall hear English travellers pronounce the name, not broad, as the natives do, but narrow, as in "cram."

Now there is an ethnological suggestion in the occurrence of the aspirate in this word *amuin* (itself probably cognate with the Latin *amnis*). In modern Gaelic and Irish it is invariably aspirated, and written *abhuinn* or *abhainn*. *B* and *m* have exactly the same sound when aspirated—viz., that of *v* or *w*; so the more correct form would be *amhuinn*. The Annals of Ulster describe how King Ecgfrid, after the battle of Dún Nechtain, where he routed the Picts, burnt *Tula Aman*, at the junction of the Almond with the Tay, in the year 686. In the 'Cronicon Elegiacum' the same river is spelt differently in three different manuscripts, one of which is in the Bodleian Library, the other two in the British Museum — namely, Amon, Aven, and Awyne. The first of these is the archaic, unaspirated form; and occurring as it does within the territory of the Northern Picts, it suggests that the old word was preserved in Pictish speech after the Scots had adopted the softened form *avon*. This is confirmed by the occurrence of the old word within the limits of Manann Gotodin, the district between Edinburgh and Stirling, formerly the land of the Southern Picts. The county of Linlithgow is bounded on the east by the Almond, on the west by the Avon—names with exactly the same meaning, one representing the older, the other the newer form of *amuin*, a river. It is remarkable that the older form is preserved in Almond Castle, which stands on the Avon; and that the river itself used to be called *mór amhuinn*, the great stream, is shown by the name of the parish—Muiravonside.

Amuin, having been softened to *amhuinn*, has given names to innumerable Avons and Evans in England, Scotland, and Ireland. But in the last-named country the aspirate had eaten away so much of the consonant before names came to be written down in English that the *mh* had to be represented by *w*, and Awn or Owen are commoner river-names in Ireland than Avon.

I am now going to submit to your attention a point which seems to have altogether escaped the notice of *most* writers on topographical etymology, and to have been undervalued even by those whose

Stress.

attention has been drawn to it. Professor Mackinnon, in a series of admirable papers on Place-Names and Personal Names in Argyle, which appeared in the 'Scotsman' newspaper in 1887, did indeed lay it down as a cardinal rule that in compound names the stress always falls on the qualitative syllable, or on the first syllable of the qualitative word; but subsequent writers, though they have referred to this rule, have almost totally disregarded it, and made guesses at derivations utterly irrespective of this trustworthy finger-post.

Now, among all the keys to the interpretation of place-names, I know of none so constant and so useful as this. I propose, therefore, to enter somewhat fully into its examination.

Place-names are either simple, as Blair (*blár*, a plain), Avon (*amhuin*, a river), Drem, Drum, or Drymen (*druim* or *dromán*, a ridge), or (which is far more usual) compound, formed of a substantive or generic term, preceded or followed by a qualitative or specific word, the latter being either an adjective, as in Anglo-Saxon Greènlaw—*gréne hlæw*, and in Gaelic Barglàss, with the same meaning; or a substantive in the oblique case, as Allerbeck, near Ecclefechan—A.S. *alr becc*, or Norse *ölr bekk*, the alder stream, and Pulfèrn, in the Stewartry of Kirkcudbright, which is the Gaelic *pol fearn* with exactly the same meaning.

This rule holds good in ordinary compounds as well as in place-names: thus, "hùsband," adopted from the Scandinavian *hús*, a house, *búandi*, one inhabiting; "plòughman," "pàncake," where "hús," "plough," and "pan," being the descriptive, specific, or qualitative syllables, sustain the stress. Fashion has modified its effect in a few such words as "goodmàn," but the personal name Goòdman or Gòdman retains the stress in the original place.

It is exceedingly difficult to find exceptions to this rule in the local—that is, the correct—pronunciation of Scottish names. After patient investigation, I have only succeeded in finding one. Professor Mackinnon says that Tiree (*tìr idhe*, cornland) has come to be pronounced by the natives of that island Tìrie (*teèry*). There will, of course, come to your mind the name Buccleùch. Heraldry has lent its sanction to the popular etymology—buck cleuch—just as in the neighbourhood of Buccleùch are to be found the Doe-cleugh, the Wolf-cleuch and the Hare-cleuch; but the position of the stress is enough to convince me that this well-known name has nothing to do with a buck, and I am strengthened in this by early spellings, which give Balcleuch.

Again, the Rev. James B. Johnston, author of an interesting book on Scottish place-names, has reminded me that Kinloch as a place-name sometimes bears the stress on the first syllable—*cinn locha*, at the head of a lake—whereas, according to this rule, it should apparently fall on the last, *locha* being the qualitative. The explanation of that is simple: the real qualitative has dropped off, as Kinloch-Rànnoch, Kinloch-Mòidart, Kinloch-Làggan, and the stress being thereby disengaged falls on the most convenient syllable, irrespectively of the meaning. Scotsmen always pronounce the personal name Kinlòch.

The neglect of this rule has led astray more than one painstaking writer. There is a site of an ancient chapel in the parish of Dailly, in Ayrshire, called Macherakìll. In the 'Old Statistical Account' it is referred to as "probably dedicated to St Macarius," a suggestion adopted and confirmed by Chalmers, and reiterated by a recent writer. But to bear this interpretation the stress must have been on the syllables "Macher," and the name would certainly have been cast in the form Kilmàchar. The fact is, that it has no reference whatever to the saint commemorated in the parishes of Old and New Machar in Aberdeen, which formed of old the *Ecclesia beati Sti Machorii;* the original dedication of this Ayrshire site has been forgotten; the place has been named in pure Gaelic (which was spoken in the neighbourhood as late as the Reformation) *machaire cill,* the field of the chapel—kirk-field.

The certainty of this rule regulating the stress in compounds condemns the derivations suggested by Mr Johnston for Alloway, Mènstrie, Mòchrum, and many others. He proceeds on pure conjecture when he gives *allt na bheath,* stream of the birches, for Alloway; *magh sratha,* plain of the strath (a pleonasm), for Mènstrie; *magh chrom,* crooked plain, for Mòchrum. These names, had such been their etymology, would assuredly have been pronounced Allowày, Menstrìe, and Mochrùm. Nor can this writer's explanation of Càllander as *coill an tìr*, wood of the land, be judged more favourably; for not only is the stress on the first syllable, but no man in his senses would so name a place. The utmost that can be done with Callander is to identify it doubtfully with Calithros, latinised Calatria, where, in 638, Donald Brec, King of Dalriada, was defeated by the Britons; and any suggestion as to its meaning must at present be pure conjecture.

In Scotland, where the majority of names are Celtic, the incidence of stress upon the qualitative has had a marked effect upon the pronunciation of Scottish as compared with English names. In Celtic speech the substantive generally, though not always, precedes the adjective or qualifying word. This tends to throw the stress in compounds upon the ultimate or penultimate. But in Teutonic languages, including Anglo-Saxon and Old Norse, the opposite order prevails, and the adjective or qualitative precedes the substantive, and carries the stress forward with it. *In Celtic the generic precedes the specific.*

No better example of this need be sought than in the name of the Scottish capital, which in Teutonic speech is Edinburgh — Agned's stronghold, but in Gaelic Dunèdin.

Englishmen, accustomed to place the stress on the first part of compound names, are prone to mispronounce the names of Scottish towns. There is a well-known anecdote of a certain official in the House of Commons, who, in reading out the names of a group of Scottish burghs, managed to misplace the stress on every one of them—Dùmfries, Kirkcudbrìght, Lochmabèn, Annàn, and Sanquhàr.

<small>Exceptions to this rule.</small> There is, however, some elasticity in the position of the Gaelic adjective, and sometimes the qualitative precedes the substantive. The name last mentioned is a case in point. Sànquhar, for *sean* (shan), old, is almost invariably placed first, and so is its Welsh equivalent, *hen*. Sanquhar is *sean cathair*, the old fort, and Mr Skene has pointed out how its own name has descended to the stream on which it stands, the Cràwick; for it is to be identified with *Kaer Rywc*, Rawic's fort, mentioned in the Book of Taliessin, Crawick representing Caer Rywc, as Cramond does Caer Amain. This Rawic seems to have left his name attached to a better known place; Ròxburgh, spelt of old Rokisburh, is Rawic's burgh.

It is unfortunate for the owner of a beautiful demesne in Galloway that its name, *sean baile* (shan bally), old homestead, has become corrupted into the ridiculous form Shàmbelly. The same name appears less unhappily disguised with the aspirate as Shìnvallie and Shànvolley in Wigtownshire, Shànavallie in Cumbrae, and Shànvallie, Shànavalley, and Shànballie in Ireland. Shenvalla also occurs in the Isle of Man, and all these names mean the old farm or homestead. "Shanty," a term used to denote a tem-

General Principles. 15

porary or dilapidated hut, seems to be borrowed from the Gaelic *sean teach* (shan tyah), old house.

The movement of stress with the qualitative syllable is well shown in two Scottish hill-names—Benmòre and Mòrven, the first being *beinn mór*, the second, where the *b* is aspirated, *mór bheinn*, and both meaning "great hill." So Ardmòre in Aberdeen, Argyle, Dumbarton, and other counties—*ard mór*, the great height — becomes when transposed Mòrar, *mór ard*, in Arisaig. Glàister or Glàster is the name of various places in Arran, Ayrshire, Galloway, and Lanark: it means *glas tír*, green land; but when the adjective takes its usual place after the substantive the stress follows it, as in Barglàss, green top, in Wigtownshire. So Glàsvein, in Lochaber, is *glas bheinn* (ven), green hill, as Benglàss in Dumbartonshire is *beinn glas*.

This syllable *glas* has two meanings: as an adjective it means green or grey, probably cognate with the Latin *glaucus;* as a substantive it means a stream. Thus, Dunglàs is G. *dún glas*, green hill, but Doùglas (locally pronounced Doòglas) is *dubh glas*, the dark stream, black water, or black burn.

Not less important than the earliest forms of spelling, to the analysis of place-names, is the correct local pronunciation. But even this has to be accepted with caution, for it sometimes happens that, although the local pronunciation is slurred, the etymology has been preserved by orthography. Instances are rare in Scotland, where early written

Importance of local pronunciation.

forms are rare, but English examples are Leicester, Worcester, Cirencester, &c.

Influence of railways on pronunciation. Railways and other causes have prevailed to alter both the stress and pronunciation of some place-names. On arriving at Carstàirs Junction the traveller hears the porters shouting the name with equal stress on both syllables, whereas locally it is pronounced with due significance Carstàirs, being probably *caer Terras*, Terras' camp. A still more familiar instance is just over the Scottish Border—namely, Carlìsle, which is called in the Book of Taliessin *Caer Lliwelydd*, Lliwelydd's stronghold, and the stress on the last syllable indicates the old qualitative. But southerners always speak of it as Càrlisle, thus falsifying the true etymology.

The change of stress is still more marked in those Scottish place-names which have been adopted as surnames. So long as those who bear them remain in Scotland, they retain the old pronunciation; but as soon as they travel south, so soon is the stress thrown forward. Balfoùr and Cathcàrt are well-known family names in Scotland, but they have been anglicised into Bàlfour and Càthcart. But the Scottish pronunciation retains the original reference to the lands whence these names were derived, Balfoùr being in Fife—*baile fuar*, the cold farm; and Cathcàrt in Renfrewshire, written in 1158 Kerkert, *cath-air* or *caer Cairt*, the castle on the river Cart. The Cart is G. *caraid*, a pair—the Black and White Cart.

General Principles. 17

Readers of the 'Lay of the Last Minstrel' may seek to identify Dèlorain. They may do so on the map of Selkirkshire, but they will never hear it on the lips of a local speaker as Scott has taught us to pronounce it. It is always called Delòrain, which clearly brings out its meaning—*dal Orain*, Oran's land.

In districts whence Celtic speech has long since disappeared, it sometimes happens that the spelling of a name is altered to correspond with some fanciful meaning attributed to it; for people are ever impatient of a name which conveys no definite meaning, and are wont to twist it into some significance. Popular errors.

The Clùden is a river in the Stewartry of Kirkcudbright, and where it joins the Nith stands the beautiful ruins of Linclùden Priory. This stream has been identified by Mr Skene as the scene of *kat glutvein gueith pen coet*, the battle of Cludvein, the affair at the head of the wood, mentioned in the Book of Taliessin. This wood has left its name to the parish, Holywood, for there was afterwards a monastery founded here, called *Abbatia Sacri Nemoris*, the Abbey of the Holy Wood, and a group of eleven huge stones perhaps commemorate the battle. Before reaching the Nith, the Cluden receives the waters of the Cairn, and above the junction is named on the Ordnance map Old Water. Now, a common Gaelic word for a stream is *allt;* this coincides in sound with the Broad Scots "auld"; appar-

B

ently those who advised the English surveyor thought it more genteel to write "old," and the real significance is completely hidden by a forced interpretation.[1]

In the adjacent county of Wigtown this word *allt*, a stream, has been dealt with in the same way. There is a hill in the parish of Inch marked on the map Auld Taggart, as if named from an aged person of the name of Taggart or Mactaggart, a common surname in the district. But on the other side of the river Luce, distant only a few hundred yards, is a stream correctly marked Altaggart Burn—that is, *allt shagairt*, the priests' stream—which has been transferred with modification to the hill opposite. The *s* in *sagart*, taking the aspirate in the genitive singular, becomes silent, according to the rule of Gaelic pronunciation.

In the same county there is, in the parish of Kirkcolm, a rocky headland called on the map Droch Head. This is the Gaelic *drochaid*, a bridge, from a fanciful notion that the promontory is the beginning of a bridge to Ireland, which is plainly visible beyond the channel. A similar place, farther south in the same county, is called the Devil's Bridge, the legend being that the devil was employed to build a bridge to the Isle of Man.

This word *drochaid* appears in absurdly corrupt

---

[1] It is only fair to observe that the Ordnance surveyors are not mainly responsible for blunders of this kind. In every case the name has been received from the proprietor, and checked by consultation with other local authorities.

General Principles. 19

form in Ayrshire and Kirkcudbright, where there are farms written on the map Bardroch Wood and Bardrochwood (stress on the second syllable), both being named from bridges and not from woods.

Less pardonable was the blunder of the surveyor who, in mapping out Lewis, transcribed the Norse name Eòropie, a corruption of *eyrar by*, the beach village, into Europa Point.

This is the same deceitful process which has prevailed to give a spurious form to certain English words in common use, such as "causeway," a term which has no affinity with "way," a road, but used to be spelt *causey* and *cawsee*. It is from the Old French *caucie* (modern French *chaussée*), which is the Low Latin *calciata*, for *calciata via*, a road made with lime. Therefore "causeway" is akin to our word "chalk."

As chalk is not a substance commonly found in Scotland, I may be permitted to turn aside for a moment in order to show that one well-known Scottish town takes its name from that mineral. Kelso was formerly written Kelhou or Calchow, in Welsh Calchvynyd, the chalk hill, and the name remains attached to the calcareous hill near the town, still called the Chalk Heugh.

The exasperating ingenuity of English Ordnance surveyors in polishing up Scottish place-names to suit English lips and ears, whereby such good Saxon names as Brigton and Langton appear figged out as Bridgeton and Longtown, has its parallel in the

Explanatory myths.

unprincipled invention of popular legends to explain names which convey no meaning to persons speaking a different language. Mr Tylor has shown how in all countries place-names are liable to fictitious interpretation. Among others he mentions the mythical derivation supplied for Exeter, which local pundits have explained by declaring that the Romans, when they first came in sight of the land where the city now stands, exclaimed, " Ecce terra ! " —" Land ho ! "

The place called Pennycomequick in Cornwall has been the subject of a very silly explanation, which is more acceptable to the general public than the pure Cornish *pen y cum cuig*, head of the cuckoo's glen. No etymology is too childish or far-fetched to find acceptance with people who have none better to offer. They would rather believe what is untrue than have nothing to believe.

<small>Origin of the name " Scot."</small>

There is no certainty about the meaning of the name Scot, designating the Dalriadic colony which left Ulster towards the close of the fifth century and occupied Cowal, Lorn, Kintyre, and Jura under Fergus Mor the son of Erc; but at all events we may utterly discard the flattering legend which made them descendants of Scotta, a daughter of Pharaoh. In Cormac's glossary the word is given as " Scuit," and " scuite " is translated " a wanderer " in O'Reilly's dictionary. Ammianus Marcellinus notices them a century before they finally settled in Argyle as " Scotti per diversa vagantes "—the

Scots wandering hither and thither, and attacking the Roman province in alliance with the Picts. Gildas, after describing this first incursion of Scots and their occupation of part of Alban (which we now call Scotland) for eight years, speaks of them as "impudentes grassatores Hiberni"—"shameless vagabonds from Ireland." They were a restless race of marauders, and may well have earned the name of *scuite*, vagabonds; and this, rather than the romantic connection with Pharaoh's daughter, seems to be the origin of the name of Scot, of which we have now so much reason to be proud.

The same process of coining derivations is at work to this day. Not long ago I read in a Wigtownshire newspaper a letter purporting to give the origin of Blàdenoch, a river in that county. On its banks is a remarkable monumental circle of great stones, which local tradition affirms to be, not druidical, as is usually believed of such monuments, but the burial-place of a native king. It is called King Galdus's tomb. Mr Skene has shown cause for crediting the story, and for believing that Gwallawg ap Lleenag, whom Tacitus called Galdus, is buried here. The writer of the letter referred to gravely asserted that Galdus, having routed his enemy in a great battle, pursued them to the banks of the Bladenoch, where, weary of slaughter, he halted his troops, crying out, "Bluid eneugh, bluid eneugh!" That King Galdus did not speak Broad Scots was nothing to this wiseacre, who had started a falsehood

22 Scottish Land-Names.

which, it is likely enough, will find currency in the neighbourhood.

Confusion of tongues. Less deliberate, because unintentional, but not the less misleading, is the fancy which altered the name of the mountain next Helvellyn into Fàirfield. The original name is Norse—*fœr fjall*, sheep-hill. So Fàirgirth on the Kirkcudbright coast is *fœr garðr*, sheepfold, as Gàdgirth in Ayrshire is *geit garðr*, the goat-pen. This word *fœr*, sheep, enters into a number of names, and is generally misinterpreted by English geographers. Thus Fair Isle, half-way between Orkney and Shetland, is a semi-translation of *fœr ey*, sheep-island, a name which appears as Fàray, one of the Orkney group, and in the plural as the Fàroe Islands, from *fœr eyjar*, sheep-islands. Similarly the Norse *geit*, a goat, and the Anglo-Saxon *gat*, are liable to confusion with *geat*, an opening, door, way, and the Broad Scots *gate*, meaning a road. But Gàtehope in Peeblesshire is *geit hof*, goat-shelter, either in Norse or Anglo-Saxon, for the two languages are almost identical in these words; and Gàteheugh on the Tweed, opposite Old Melrose, is the goat's height, exactly corresponding in meaning to Ardgòur in Argyle, *ard gobhar* (gowr).

A few miles lower down the Tweed, on the Merton Water, a grey crag rears itself over the stream. This is written in the map Craig Over, as if from its position towering over the stream. But it is a map-maker's blunder: he took the real name Craigòwer as being Broad Scots for "over," and improved it accordingly. The real name is Gaelic, *creag odhar* (owr), grey craig, or *creag gobhar* (gowr), goat's crag. There is another instance of this name not far from Edinburgh, at Liberton, where the map-maker has made it Craigo'er. Just so Glenòver and Drumòver in Ayrshire are doubtless *gleann odhar* (owr), grey or dun glen, and *druim odhar*, grey ridge, as Corròur in Perthshire stands for *coire odhar*, grey or dun corry, to distinguish it from green corries.

To select an example of forced meaning from the other extremity of Scotland—no doubt Cape Wrath is associated in the popular mind with the fury of the gales that rage round it, and its present spelling is owing to that idea. But the Norse name was *hvarf*, a turning-point. In Pont's map it is written Faro Head, another attempt at phonetic spelling; and close by he gives Row na farrif—that is, *rudha na atharrachaidh* (aharrahy), point of the turning—which appears in our modern maps as Farout Head. In a book published in 1583, of which only two perfect copies are known to exist, 'La Navigation du Roi d'Escosse, Jaques cinquième du nom, autour de son royaume,' Cape Wrath is thus described, "Wraith Hotherwise, nommé Fairhead, c'est à dire Belle Pointe ou beau Cap;" whereby the author, compiling his work from English notes, led his readers to believe that the headland was called Wraith Hotherwise.

In studying place-names, in order to obtain a true picture of the state of the land which they describe,

Exaggeration.

one must take into account that tendency to magnify
the importance of localities and individuals which
is so common in all rural districts. All nomenclature is comparative, and when the field of comparison is limited, undue value is bestowed upon degrees
of excellence which would be scarcely perceptible
in a wider field.

The unconscious pride which, among Celtic tribes,
exalted the chief into a *righ*, or king, may be traced
in other terms of Celtic speech. This *righ*, for example, would naturally choose the best spot for
his dwelling, and in our latitude the best spot is
that which receives most sunshine. Hence *grianán*
(greenan), a sunny place, from *grian* (green), the
sun, is described by O'Brien as a royal seat or
palace—" and this," says Dr Joyce, " is unquestionably
its meaning when it occurs in topographical names."
But, in truth, it often has a much humbler origin;
and Greenan in Ayrshire and Bute, Grennan, Argren-
nan, and Bargrennan in Galloway and Dumfriesshire, though perhaps commemorative of a chief's
abode, may also bear the interpretation assigned to
grianán in modern Gaelic dictionaries—a drying-
place for anything, particularly peats.

Ambiguous meanings. Furthermore, there is the difficulty arising from
ambiguity. Many meanings are often attached to
the same word either simultaneously or by successive
generations. The syllable "ark" is a very frequent
suffix in place-names, and no doubt it often represents the Gaelic word *earc;* but even when that

origin has been arrived at, one is still left in doubt as to the real meaning, for in O'Reilly's Irish dictionary that word is interpreted—"water; the sun; any beast of the cow kind; a salmon; a bee; honey; a tax; heaven; a rainbow; red; speckled."

More than this, even of those names which admit of intelligible explanation, many must be rendered as if followed by a note of interrogation in brackets. I can best illustrate this by an example from Irish topography. There is a townland near Ennis called Clonroad, and no objection could have been taken to explaining it as *cluain ród*, the meadow by the roadside, for that is precisely the form which those words would assume in composition. But it so happens that, in the Annals, Ennis is usually called *Inis cluana-ramhfhoda*—that is, the inch or pasture of the meadow of the long rowing. Here the original name has been divided between two places, Ennis representing *inis*, the pasture, and Clonroad the *cluan ramhfhoda*, the meadow of the long rowing or boatrace. In this compound *ramhfhoda*, the *m* and *f* are silenced by so-called aspiration, and the result is the sound "roada."

[margin: Names not always what they seem.]

There is no key provided to the analysis of Scottish place-names as there is in Ireland by a plentiful early literature, so it is well to bear in mind this example of the necessity for rejecting a simple and obvious explanation for a complicated and obscure one. But it would be unpardonable to take this course except upon clear documentary evidence.

It may, perhaps, be thought that I have devoted too much time to pointing out errors and dwelling on difficulties; but one of the first tasks to be undertaken by the student of place-names is the detection and demolition of fictitious etymologies: one of the last lessons he can hope to convey is that where no certain evidence—documentary, oral, or physical—can be had as to the origin of a name, the only right thing to do is to leave it unexplained.

LECTURE II.

THE LANGUAGES OF SCOTTISH PLACE-NAMES.

TRACES OF PRE-CELTIC SPEECH—THE IVERIAN OR SILURIAN RACE—THE FIRBOLG OF THE IRISH ANNALISTS—THE ERNAI—THE TWO MAIN BRANCHES OF CELTIC SPEECH—OBSOLETE WORDS—THE OPERATION OF *UMLAUT*—LINGUISTIC CHANGE—EFFECTS OF ASPIRATION AND ECLIPSE—DIFFERENCE BETWEEN GAELIC AND WELSH—Q CELTS AND P CELTS—TEST WORDS—SIMILARITY OF GAELIC AND WELSH—GHOST-NAMES.

AVING dwelt in the first lecture on the general principles to be observed in the study of place-names, and pointed out some of the chief snares to be guarded against in the endeavour to read their true meaning, attention may now be given to the different languages in which such names are found in Scotland.

Leaving out of account those framed in modern English or that form of Old Northern English which survives in Broad Scots, which generally explain themselves, the rest may be assumed to have been conferred by people speaking one of the following languages or dialects:—

1. Pre-Celtic . Iverian or Silurian.
2. Celtic, either { Goidelic or Gaelic.
   Brythonic, Cymric, or Welsh.
   Pictish.
3. Old Norse.
4. Anglo-Saxon.

Besides these there are a few, but very few, names altered from the Latin of the Roman conquerors. Considering that the Roman occupation of Southern Scotland lasted for more than three centuries, it may be matter for wonder that they failed to impress their language upon the nomenclature of that country, especially when the extent to which the Norsemen have done so is taken into account. But the fact is that, although Latin was the official language of the Romans, the legions were latterly recruited mainly from nations whose speech was not Latin. The Second and Sixth Legions, which remained longest in the northern province, were drawn principally from Gaul and Spain; hence almost the only names which commemorate them are military technical terms, such as *castrum*, a camp, which occurs as Chester and Chesters in the counties of Dumfries, Dumbarton, Roxburgh, Berwick, Mid and East Lothian, and Fife.

Christian missionaries, of course, introduced a number of Latin ecclesiastical terms, which became part of the Gaelic or Welsh languages, such as Gaelic *eaglais*, Welsh *eglwys*, from *ecclesia*, a church, which gives the name to Eccles, near Coldstream, and again near Thornhill, in Dumfriesshire; and to Ecclefèchan, in Dumfriesshire, the church of St Fechan or Vigean, who died in 664. Close to Ecclefechan the same word appears in Eàglesfield, and again near Paisley, in Eàglesham. Lesmahàgow is a corruption of *eaglais Machute*, St Machutus' church.

Easbog, a bishop, the Gaelic rendering of *episcopus*, gives such names as Gillèspie, a farm in Wigtownshire—that is, *cill easpuig*, the bishop's cell or chapel, not to be confused, though identical in form, with the surname Gillespie, which means *giola easpuig*, the bishop's servant. Indeed *cill* itself (pronounced *keel*), so characteristic of Gaelic names in Scotland and Ireland in the prefix Kil, is a loan word from the Latin, being the locative case of *ceall*, a cell or chapel, from the Latin *cella*.

Next to nothing is known of the language spoken by the people—presumably non-Aryan—who inhabited this country before the coming of the Celts; and of the people themselves we have little certain information, though the ancient annals of Ireland teem with notices of them, and though they have been the subject of much speculation and scrutiny in modern times. But inasmuch as some of the place-names we pronounce at this day are probably remains of the speech of this race, an attempt must be made to review briefly what has been ascertained about them. *Pre-Celtic, Iverian, or Silurian.*

The early Irish historical legends were collected

in the sixteenth century by Michael O'Clery, one of the compilers of the 'Annals of the Four Masters,' and put in the form of a consecutive narrative, called the 'Leabhar Gabhala,' or 'Book of Conquests.' All through this book mention is made of a small, dark-haired race of men, whose fate it was to be continually getting out of the way of stronger people. These have been identified, more or less hypothetically, with the long-skulled people whose remains are found in Great Britain and Western Europe in long barrows with galleries and chambers, doubtfully distinguished by the shape of their skulls from the round-headed people, who buried in round cairns and grave-mounds. The facts that no metal, except gold, has ever been found in the long barrows, that pottery is extremely rare, and that weapons and implements of stone are of common occurrence, go some way to justify the conclusion arrived at by Canon Greenwell and Mr Boyd Dawkins, that the people who buried in this peculiar way were still in the neolithic or polished-stone grade of civilisation.

Yet if it may be supposed that this is the people described by the Greek writers who first make mention of Britain, some tribes of them, at all events, held together long enough to form an important mining community in Cornwall. A well-known passage in Diodorus Siculus, who wrote in the last century before Christ, thus refers to them :—

Those who dwell near the promontory of Britain [the Land's End], which is called Belerion, are singularly fond of strangers, and, from their intercourse with foreign merchants, are singularly civilised in their habits. These people obtain the tin by skilfully working the soil which produces it; this, being rocky, has earthy interstices, in which, working the ore, and then fusing, they reduce it to metal, and when they have formed it into cubical shapes, they convey it to a certain island lying off Britain, called Ictis; for at the low tide the intervening space being laid dry, they carry thither the tin in great abundance.

Now, if Diodorus was as careful in his statements regarding the ethnology of Belerion as he was in describing its topography and mineralogy, it would appear that he is here dealing with a tribe of the pre-Celtic population, already confined to the limits of the south-western promontory by the advance of the Celts, but raised by contact with civilised traders far above the level of their fellow-countrymen. The two names, Belerion and Ictis, may represent Diodorus' attempt to render phonetically the pre-Celtic names attached to the Land's End and St Michael's Mount.

In the 'Leabhar Gabhala' mention is made of a people called the Firbolg, who are said to have arrived in Ireland about a thousand years after the flood. They were the descendants of Simon Breac, and had been enslaved by the Greeks, who made them dig earth and carry it in leather bags. Now the Irish for "bag" is *bolg*, and *firbolg* means the men with bags—bagmen.

There were with them men called *fir domhnan*, because of the *domhin*, or pits, which they dug, as well as others called *fir gaillian*, or spearmen, from the *gai*, or spears, with which they guarded the others while they worked. They had possession of Ireland, it is said, until they were driven out with great slaughter by the *Tuatha de Danaan* after the battle of Muigh Tuireadh. We seem to have here the dim record of a disappearing race, and these bagmen and pitmen, as Mr Skene pointed out, were probably Iverian or Silurian miners from Cornwall, driven thence by the stronger Celtic population to take refuge in Ireland, where they attempted to carry on their native industry—the only one known to them.

Without putting too much stress upon these hazy traditions, it is clear that in various parts of Ireland and Scotland there are traces of a black-haired, black-eyed race, differing in a marked degree from the larger limbed and brown or fair haired people who form the bulk of the population, and generally held in low esteem by any other race which happened to be dominant.

Thus in the preface to M'Firbis' 'Book of Genealogies' we read:—

Every one who is white of skin, brown of hair, bold, honourable, daring, prosperous, bountiful in the bestowal of prosperity, wealth, and rings, and is not afraid of battle,—they are the descendants of the sons of Miledh (the Milesians) in Erin. Every one who is fair-haired, vengeful, large, and every plunderer; every musical person; the professor of musical and entertaining performances, who are adepts in all Druidical and magical arts,—they are the descendants of the Tuatha de Danaan in Erin. Every one who is black-haired, who is a tattler, guileful, tale-telling, noisy, contemptible; every wretched, mean, strolling, unsteady, harsh, and inhospitable person; every slave, every low thief, every churl, every one who loves not to listen to music and entertainment, the disturbers of every council and assembly, and the promoters of discord among the people,—these are the descendants of the Firbolg. . . . This is taken from an old book.

From this and many passages of similar import in the early chronicles, it may be gathered that the black-haired Iverians, known as Firbolg and Silures, were the earliest inhabitants of this country of which any trace remains; that they were akin to the Basque population of our own day, and had the physical characteristics of the river-drift men. They must have distinguished one locality from another by means of place-names in their own language, and no doubt some of these names still remain in our maps, just as in Australasia many native names will remain, interspersed among those of English origin, ages after the aborigines shall have ceased to be known as a distinct people.

But whereas the Australian aborigines have been dispossessed by a literary people, capable of writing down phonetically the native names of places, the Iverians were ousted by a people who could not even write their own language. The old names, or some of them, would be transmitted orally; but what chance is there of our interpreting their meaning at this day, after centuries of detrition and linguistic corruption? Even where, in a few cases, careful students have detected a probability that certain Scottish place-names are of Iverian origin, there exist no grounds for so much as a guess at their meaning, and one is fain to content one's self with the prudent observation of Cormac Mac Cuillenain, an etymologist of the ninth century, who, though not himself averse to hazarding the wildest shots at derivations, remarked: " It is not every syllable that receives interpretation. Therefore let no one wonder how *parn* comes to mean a whale, *et alia similia*."

The best chance of recovering the form of Iverian names occurs in those rare instances where a record has been preserved of the names successively borne by some prominent natural feature, like the great rock guarding the entrance to the Clyde, of which the earliest recorded name is Nemhtur or Nevtur.[1] This may have been a phonetic rendering by the Gael or Pict of the Iverian name of a noted stronghold.[2] After the decisive victory of the Welsh prince and Christian champion, Rydderch Hael, at the battle

[1] Rosnèath = *ros Nemhedh* (nevey), the headland of Nemhedh, may be compared with Nevtur. The parish of Rosneath is called Neueth and Neyt in the *Reg. de Passelet* (pp. 114 and 308). About 1225 the land is called Nemhedh in a charter of Earl Alwin in favour of Maldoven, dean of Lennox (*Reg. de Levenad*, p. 20), and in 1264 Nevyd (*Compota Camerarii*, vol. i. p. 47).

[2] If, however, Nevtur be a Celtic name, it would bear the interpretation *naomh* (nave) *tor*, holy tower or rock.

Their Languages.   35

of Ardderyd (now Arthuret) on the Dumfriesshire Esk in A.D. 573, this rock of Nevtur became the seat of government of the Britons of Strathclyde, and was called by them Alclut, the cliff on the Clyde; but to the Gaelic tribes around it was known as *dùn Bretann*, the Britons' fortress. When Gaelic speech once more overflowed the Welsh in Strathclyde, that name was confirmed, and now, and probably for evermore, it is called Dumbàrton.

But although in the present state of our knowledge it is not possible to assign meanings to the scraps of pre-Celtic speech which, like Belerion, Ictis, and Nevtur, seemed to have survived the lapse of time and ethnological change, it is reasonable to keep an eye on certain names as not improbably of Iverian origin.

The first syllable of the name Ireland is a contracted form of the name Iver, Emer, Eber, or Eire, which was very likely a pre-Celtic vocable. Adopted into Gaelic speech, it received the genitive case Eirinn, the favourite name for Ireland, just as Alban, the ancient name of Scotland, is the genitive case of Alba.

This name Eire, as Professor Rhys has shown,[1] seems to have been specially applied to the people of Munster, whose capital appears in early Irish MSS. as Temair Erand, or Tara of the Erna (or Iverians). In Welsh it appears as Iwerddon, and in some of the early MS. editions of Juvenal it is writ-

[1] Rhind Lectures, 1889.

ten Iuverna, Iberna, and Juberna. The form Iuverna corresponds exactly with the Iuverna or Iwwerna of the earliest Ogam inscriptions in Ireland and Wales.

It is impossible to deal with Scottish place-names without allusion to the changes which have taken place in those of Ireland, a country whence the ethnology and language of Scotland were repeatedly recruited in early times. And what lends special importance to this name Iver or Emer, apparently the designation of a notable branch of the pre-Celtic race, is the fact that it occurs in the middle of Scotland. *Sraith Hirend*, now Strathèarn, can hardly be other than the vale of the Erann or Iverians, commemorating, probably, a settlement of the same people from whom Lough Erne, in Ireland, is said to have taken its name. We are told in the 'Annals of the Four Masters' that in the year B.C. 1443 Fiacha Labhrainne, King of Ireland, defeated "the Ernai, a sept of the Firbolg, on the plain where Lough Erne now is. After the battle was gained from them, the lake flowed over them, so that it is from them that the lake is named—that is, a lake over the Ernai."

All the names by which Ireland was known in ancient poetry — namely, Eire, Banba, Fodla, and Elga—seem to be reflected in the Scottish place-names Earn, Banff, Athole (Ath Fotla), Elgin, and Glenelg, and Professor Rhys inclines to regard these names as being in the Iverian language.

Mr Skene has drawn attention to the frequent occurrence of the syllable *Il* in the topography of the Basque province, and, recalling the legend of the occupation of Islay by the Firbolg, suggests that the name of that island, as well as that of the two rivers called Isla in Banff and Forfar, the Ulie in Sutherland (written Ila by Ptolemy), and other rivers called Ale, Elwan, and Allan, there may be recognised an Iverian word. There is perhaps more significance in the resemblance he traces between *ur*, the Basque word for water, and our river names Urr, Oure, Ourin, and Ore. He adds Ure and Urie; but these are undoubtedly Gaelic, from the yew-tree—viz., *amhuinn iubhar* (avon yure), stream of the yews, and *amhuinn iubharaich* (yureh), stream of the yew-wood. Compare with these Palnùre in Kirkcudbrightshire—that is, *pol na' iubhar*, stream of the yews—and Glenure, in Argyleshire, the glen of yews.

But it avails not to dwell longer on a subject which involves such bare speculation. The most hopeful means of arriving at a recognition of pre-Celtic names would be to prepare a list for every parish in Scotland of names which cannot be explained in any Celtic or Teutonic speech. This has never yet been done, though scholars have been eager enough to collect names capable of explanation: but it is in the irreducible residuum that careful comparison might produce something like an acquaintance with Iverian nomenclature.

Celtic.

I now turn to the consideration of that language in the various dialects of which the majority of Scottish place-names are cast. Here we are on much firmer ground, though it has indeed been grievously undermined by the wild guesswork of Celtic enthusiasts.

The Celtic language, in which such a large proportion of Scottish names is formed, consists of two main branches—the Goidelic and the Brythonic, which, for convenience, may be referred to as Gaelic and Welsh. But it must be understood that these terms are here used in a general sense, not as restricted by modern use. In Gaelic are included the various dialects still spoken in Ireland, Man, and the Highlands of Scotland, *as well as their archaic forms;* and in Welsh is comprehended not only the living language of Wales, but that form of it which was once current over the whole of the west of England and part of Scotland, in a chain of territory, broken only by the Gaelic or Pictish province of Galloway, extending from the Land's End on the south to the Firth of Clyde on the north.

In those districts where these languages are still spoken, the interpretation of names is generally as easy to a Celtic scholar as it is for an Englishman to read the meanings of names formed in English. The only circumstances likely to baffle either of them is one of those following:—

Obsolete words.

First, The occurrence of obsolete words — words which have fallen out of use or have altered from the old form. *Bréach* (bragh) is a disused name for a wolf, unknown in modern Gaelic, and closely resembling *breac* (brack), spotted, brindled, or streaked, and *breac*, a trout; but it is not improbably the specific syllable in Bràco, the name of a place in Perthshire and another in Aberdeen. It appears to be the same name as Breagho in Fermanagh, which the Irish annalists render *Bréagh mhagh* (vah)—that is, wolf-field. Yet a modern Gaelic student would not recognise the word, because it is not in the living language.

Ar means ploughed land, but it also means slaughter; so the Gaelic names Knocknàr and Barràer, which occur in Galloway, may signify either the slaughter-hill, the battle-hill, or the ploughed hill. Equivoques.

Second, The operation of the law of *umlaut*, as German philologers call it, whereby the vowel sound in one syllable is altered by the vowel sound in a syllable following, as hŭsband and nŏstril stand for hōūse-band and nōse-thrill. An instance of this in a Celtic place-name is Slamànnan, for *sliabh* (slieve or slew) *Manann*, the moor of the Picts of Manann. Among Saxon names an extreme example of the action of *umlaut* is the name of Ruthwell, a parish in Dumfriesshire, locally pronounced Rìvvell, but being really Rood Well, for so the holy well there was named from the rood or cross—the Ruthwell Cross, so well known to antiquaries. Umlaut.

Linguistic change.

Third, Linguistic change in the pronunciation of vocables. *Cnoc* is an ancient term denoting a hill, and it is so written in modern Gaelic dictionaries, but no Highlander would understand what it meant, for it has come to be pronounced *crochd*. There is evidence that this change has taken place within the last three centuries and a half. Gaelic was spoken in the mountainous parts of Galloway as late as the days of Queen Mary. In a list of Galloway place-names which I prepared some years ago, upwards of 240 began with the syllable Knock, and only one with that of Crock. The single exception was Crockencàlly, near Kirkbean; it was church-land of old, and the name Ladyland, occurring close by, confirmed the obvious meaning *cnocán cailleach*, the nuns' hillock. This seems to show that the change of *cnoc* into *crochd* was just beginning to take place at the time Gaelic was dying out in Galloway.

But why should a change, apparently so arbitrary, take place, of changing *n* into *r*? For the same reason that we English-speaking folk sound "nock" instead of "knock." It requires a conscious effort to begin a word with *kn*, and the whole tendency of linguistic change is to get rid of exertion. The Gael, as we shall see presently, is very partial to *k:* he belongs to the Q group of Celts, and cannot be persuaded to give up his beloved gutturals; so instead of dropping the *k*, as we have done, he kept it, and altered the *n* into the easier sound of *r*. Thus

Crochrìoch, the name of several small hills in Argyleshire, is the same as Knockrèoch, which occurs in Galloway, and both were originally *cnoc riabhach* (reeagh), the grey hill.

Lastly, One effect of aspiration and eclipse, pro- <small>Aspiration.</small> cesses to which certain consonants in Gaelic and Welsh are peculiarly liable, is to render certain words indistinguishable from each other in composition, and Professor Mackinnon has supplied a good instance of how a Gaelic scholar may be misled thereby. The bold headland on the west of Tiree is called Kenvàra, and the Ordnance surveyor, who evidently had some knowledge of Gaelic, has written it *Ceann a' bharra*, meaning the hill-head, the promontory of the hill or of the crop, for *barr* means both hill-top and crop in Gaelic. But *b* and *m* when aspirated both represent the sound of *v*, and the real sense of Kenvara is *ceann mhara*, the headland of the sea.

The same combination, without the aspirate, gives Kenmàre, in Ireland, and good Gaelic scholars might easily be misled into translating Connemàra in the same way—*ceann na mara;* but they would be wrong, for that name, as we know from the annalists, is *Conmaicne mara*, the seaside Conmaicne, the progeny of Conmac, the son of Fergus, king of Connaught.

So much for aspiration: now for an example of <small>Eclipse.</small> the perplexing effect of eclipse. There is in Galloway a ridge of land called Drummatìer. It is

on the verge of a wild mountainous tract, and
would well bear the interpretation *druim mac tire,*
ridge of the wolves, for *mac tire* (teer), signifying
" son of the soil," is an old and common name for
a wolf. But the termination -teer usually has a
different signification. The consonant *s* is liable in
composition to be silenced by aspiration and replaced
by *t*—to be eclipsed, in short; Baltier, in the same
district as Drummatier, must be interpreted *baile
t-shaoir* (bally teer), the carpenter's house, just as
Ballinteer, near Dublin and Londonderry, is *baile an
t-shaoir* (teer) with the article. Drummatier, therefore, may have nothing to do with wolves, but may
simply be *druim a' t-shaoir,* the carpenter's ridge.
Still more perplexing examples, for they are com-
bined with the change of *n* into *r*, are found in the
names Colintràive and Ardentrìve in Argyleshire.
These are places where, long before the days of
steamers, cattle were driven down from the hills
and forced to swim across a narrow part of the
loch. Colintraive is *caol an t-shnaoimh,* the strait
of the swimming, the original sound " snave " having
been altered by the so-called eclipse of *s* by *t*, and
the alteration of *n* into *r*. So Ardentrive is *ard an
t-shnaoimh,* the headland of the swimming.

The process which Celtic philologists term eclipsis
is explained by O'Donovan as " the suppression of
the sounds of certain radical consonants by prefixing
others of the same organ." The consonants said to
be subject to eclipse are—

B	eclipsed by	M	P	eclipsed by	B
C	"	G	T	"	D
D and G	"	N	and S	"	T
F	"	Bh = V			

We should probably never have heard of eclipsis but for the pedantry of early Irish writers, who seem to have been ever anxious to cram as many letters as possible into a word; and so, when a hard or surd consonant like *t* changed into the sound of a soft or sonant one like *d*, they insisted on writing both, though only the sound of *d* was heard.

"All initial consonants," writes O'Donovan, "that admit of eclipsis are eclipsed in all nouns of the genitive case plural, when the article is expressed, and sometimes even in the absence of the article."

Now, the qualitative syllable or syllables in compound Gaelic place-names often consist of a noun in the genitive plural. Thus Craigenvèoch in Wigtownshire is *creagán fitheach* (feeagh), crag of the ravens, and would be written in Irish *creagán bhfitheach*. But in reality the change from *f* to *v* is a natural and easy one, and is the ordinary outcome of the invariable tendency of speakers to avoid effort. The so-called eclipse of *c, p,* and *t* by *g, b,* and *d,* is capable of similar explanation.

But the changes of *b* into *m*, *d* and *g* into *n*, and *s* into *t*, are to be accounted for differently. Lagniemàwn, the name of a marshy field in Wigtownshire, probably represents *lag nam ban,* hollow of the women. Here *b* may with accuracy be described as having been eclipsed by the final *m* of the article. It becomes like the mute *b* (also organic) in our "lamb." But a converse process is more usual in English pronunciation, for we sound an excrescent *b* after *m* in such words as "number," "chamber," "humble," and "timber."

The eclipse of *d* and *g* by *n* occurs when these consonants are silenced by aspiration, and the final *n* of the preceding article takes their place. In the eclipse of *s* by *t*, *s* is silenced by aspiration, and a purely excrescent *t* takes its place. Bartàggart in Wigtownshire is *barr t-shagairt*, hill-top of the priest; but Balsàggart in Ayrshire represents *baile sagart*, house of the priests.

For the same reason, the personal name Mactaggart, the priest's son, never appears as Macsaggart, seeing that a man cannot claim more than one father.

<small>Distinction between Gaelic and Welsh.</small> Certain well-marked linguistic differences exist between Gaelic and Welsh, and these must be shortly stated; but it is no part of my object to attempt to decide the vexed question of their relative antiquity. Suffice it to say that almost at the remotest point to which Celtic speech can be traced, there may be recognised a preference on the part of certain tribes for labial consonants, on the part of others for guttural. Eleven hundred years ago Cormac, the Irish scribe, noted the difference between the Gaelic *mac* and the Welsh *map*, a son.

Now, this divergence was not intentional: the

original word for son was MAQVI in the genitive case; the Gaelic race, owing to some organic peculiarity, preferred the guttural Q, and their word for "son" became MAC; the Welsh, for the same reason, preferred the labial V, and their word became MAP, becoming later AP, and now often wasted away in simple P, as in the personal names Pritchard = Ap Richard, or Probert = Ap Robert, as we should say Richardson or Robertson.

Professor Rhys has made convenient use of this characteristic, and divided neo-Celtic dialects into the Q group, representing the Goidelic or Gaelic, and the P group, representing the Brythonic, Cymric, or Welsh. In Scotland, where there were, as we know, of old Gaelic-speaking and Welsh-speaking Celts, it is useful to have a few test-words in either language to apply to the analysis of place-names. One very commonly chosen for this purpose is

Gaelic, *ceann;* Welsh, *pen;* English, head.

Thus, to take two examples from the county of Ayr, which, being in the territory of the Welsh people of Strathclyde, exhibits Gaelic and Welsh names side by side, Kinchòil near Ayr means in Gaelic *cinn choill* (hoyle), at the head of the wood, *cinn* being the locative case of *ceann;* and Pencòt near Dalry is the Welsh *pen coed*, wood-head.

Pen is a word most characteristic of Welsh topography, nevertheless its occurrence among place-names is by no means sufficient to warrant the assumption of a former Welsh population. It is sometimes the corruption of another word. Thus the stream flowing past the ancient and picturesque parish church of Minigaff in Galloway is called the Penkìln, but it is not a Welsh word. In Pont's map it is spelt Poolkill, which represents the Gaelic *pol cill* (keel), water or stream of the church. That there were Welshmen—Strathclyde Britons—settled in Galloway is proved by the name Culbràtten, occurring in the next parish to Minigaff—that is, *cuil* or *cúl Breatain,* the corner or hill-back of the Welshman, and Drumbrèddan in Old Luce parish is *druim Breatain,* the Welshman's ridge; but the occurrence of such names shows that their presence was exceptional, and could not prevail to give a Welsh cast to place-names.

Another good test-word is supplied by the name of a common tree—

Gaelic, *fearn;* Welsh, *gwern;* English, alder.

Being a waterside tree, it gives its name to many rivers. The Nairn is *amhuinn* na' *fhearn* (the *f* silenced by aspiration), alder-river; but the *f* was not always silent in this name, for it is present in Strathnavern, the old spelling of Strathnairn. But in Ayrshire the Welsh name remains in Gàrnock, a river near Dalry, *afon gwernach;*[1] which is further

[1] In Welsh *f* represents our *v* sound, *ff* that of our *f* in "far."

disguised by the addition of the Scots "burn" in the name Gàrnaburn, near Colmonèll.

Gaelic, *fionn, finn;* Welsh, *gwynn;* English, white.

These words often appear in combination with Gaelic *ceann* and Welsh *pen*, a head. Thus the Welsh name Penwyn, the Pennowindos of early inscriptions, means "white head," and so does the Gaelic *ceann finn*, more often *ceann fhinn* (cann hinn, the *f* being silenced by aspiration). There is a low hill called Knockcànnon facing the ancient stronghold of the Douglas—the Threave, near Kirkcudbright. Local tradition has it that it is so named Knockcànnon because it is the place where Mons Meg, the great cannon, was planted to batter down the castle; but this is suspiciously like the usual attempt to explain a name by reference to some familiar or notable incident. Comparison with the Irish place-names Carrigcànnon, Drumcànnon, and Lettercànnon, which Dr Joyce interprets as the crag, the ridge, and the half townland (*leth tír*) of the white top, incline one to construe Knockcannon as the hill with the white top—*i.e.*, a grassy hill amid moorland or woodland. But Foilnacànnony in Tipperary and Glennacànnon in Wicklow are connected in legend with certain cows called *ceann fhionn* (cann hinn), because they had white heads.

Time permits but a cursory consideration of the

separation of the Celts into P and Q groups: it is enough for our present purpose to accept the fact that the Gaels used *c* in many words where the Welsh had *p*. But it may be remarked in passing that a similar division in labial and guttural groups prevails in other languages. Where the Tuscan Italian says *plaga* for the shore, the Neapolitan says *chiaja*; where Herodotus wrote κῶς and κότερος, other Greek writers used πῶς and πότερος.

<small>Words beginning with *sr*.</small> The combination *sr* at the beginning of a word is avoided by the people of nearly every nation; indeed it is said that, except the Irish and Scottish Gael, the only European race that can brook it is the Lithuanian. When Gaelic names came to be written in English characters, this difficulty was eased by the insertion of a dental, and so it comes that many places called Strone or Stroan represent the Gaelic *sron*, a nose, equivalent to the Norse *nes* and Anglo-Saxon *næs* (naze). Stronachlàcher on Loch Katrine is a rock of offence to English tourists: it is the Gaelic *sron a' chlachair*, the mason's headland or point. The bold headland separating the Holy Loch from Loch Long is now called Strone Point, equivalent to "Point Point"; but Stròwan and Strùan, in Perthshire and Inverness-shire, represent *sruthan* (sruhan), a diminutive or plural form of *sruth*, a stream.

The Welsh found the same difficulty as we do in beginning a word with *sr*, but they got rid of the difficulty somewhat differently. Instead of turning the Gaelic *srath* into strath, they made it *ystrad*, which is probably the origin of Yèster in Haddingtonshire; and this word appears in the twelfth century in an obsolete name for Annandale, Estrahannent. In *sron* they dropped the *s* altogether, substituting *t*, and made it *trwyn*, the regular Welsh word for "a nose." This is the origin of the Ayrshire seaport Troon, the point, written in Pont's map "The Truyn."

If the Latin *planum*, level ground, has no affinity to the Gaelic *lann*, ground, Welsh *llan*, an enclosure, and specially a church, and English *lawn* (which Professor Skeat seems to imply by his silence on the subject), at all events they run very closely together. Carmìchael, in Lanarkshire, is written Planmichael in an Inquisition of David I. In Celtic speech the initial *p* soon dropped off: the special meaning of the Wesh *llan*, a church, was forgotten, and it has been altered in our maps to Long Newton, Long Niddrie, and Longformacus, because the map-makers thought they had in *llan* the vulgar Scots "lang" for "long." Similarly, in Cumberland and Yorkshire we find such names as Long Newton and Longmarton. But in Pictish Forfarshire it was the *l* that dropped out and the *p* that remained, leaving Panmùre and Panbrìde, the great church and the church of St Bridget or Bride.

The Welsh word *llanerch*, a forest glade, has suffered corruption by the officiousness of geogra-

D

phers in the same way as *llan*. It remains unchanged in the county name Lànark, which is supposed to be referred to in the Book of Carmarthen:—

"Awallen peren atif in llanerch"—
Sweet apple-tree that grows in Lanark.

Lànrick and Drumlànrig are little altered forms of *llanerch* (the latter being a hybrid of Gaelic and Welsh); but in Whitburn parish, Linlithgowshire, the village which used to be called Lànrig has been metamorphosed on our maps into Longridge.

Similarity of Gaelic and Welsh.
The attempt to distinguish between those of our place-names which originated with a Gaelic people on the one hand and a Welsh one on the other is interfered with by the identity of many vocables in the two languages. The Welsh did not always use *p* where the Gaels preferred *k*. Three of the commonest generic terms in Gaelic place-names are *cathair* (caher), a camp or fort; *carn*, a cairn or heap—a hill; and *carraig*, a crag, represented in Welsh spelling by *caer*, *carn*, and *careg*.

Names compounded of these and many other words—such as Gaelic *mór*, Welsh *maur*, great; Gaelic *inis*, Welsh *ynys*, an island; Gaelic *amhuinn*, Welsh *afon*, a river—may belong to either of the two languages. Càrrick, for example, the ancient earldom of South Ayrshire, may be Welsh, for it is in Strathclyde, where Welsh was once the vernacular; but it is just as likely to be Gaelic, for there are numberless Càrricks in Ireland, where Welsh was

never spoken. But there are certain words in each
dialect which are not found in the other. There is
no commoner generic word in Gaelic topography
than *druim*, a ridge, which, so far as I know, hardly
enters into Welsh place-names; its place is supplied
by *cefn*, and this vocable is easily recognised in
Giffen, the name of two places in Ayrshire, one
near Dalry, the other near Beith. A still better
known example is the suburb of Glasgow called
Gòvan, which, although we write it with an *o*, was
written Guven in 1147, and probably means "the
ridge." [1]

Cuff Hill, a prominent ridge, 675 feet high, in
North Ayrshire, seems to be another corruption of
the same word.

The few minutes which remain to me are too
short to enter upon consideration of Pictish names,
so I may devote them to bringing to your notice a
strange effect that literature sometimes has upon
place-names, bringing about a permanent alteration
of form by means of a copyist's blunder.

Ghost-names.

There exist in Scotland three well-known examples
of this kind of accident, aptly classed by Canon Isaac
Taylor as "ghost-names." Dr Reeves first detected
the blunder of a copyist in the name Iona. This

---

[1] It has been pointed out to me that Govan is not on a ridge of
land. To this I must answer that there are ridges all round it,
and that names often slipped from high land to low, as *allt* has
come to mean a glen, and the stream in the glen; and many hills
are known as the Lag or the Laggan, from the *lag* or hollow at the
foot of the hill.

island was originally called I (pronounced *ee*), also written Hii, Hye, Ia, Iou, Yi, and Y, meaning "island," a word no longer in modern Gaelic, but retained in medieval Gaelic, as *i Coluim cille*—the island of Columba of the Church. Adamnan, in his 'Life of St Columba,' makes a Latin adjective out of I, and writes *Ioua insula:* some copyist mistaking *u* for *n*, wrote *Iona insula*, and the error has been perpetuated in the romantic name by which the island is now known.

In another instance *u* was mistaken for *m*. Tacitus, in his 'Life of Agricola,' describes how the Caledonians under Galgacus were drawn up on the *Mons Graupius*. This was copied *Grampius*, and transferred to the great ridge Drumalban, *dorsum Albaniæ*, or backbone of Scotland, which is therefrom known now as the Grampian Mountains. The name Drumalban has itself disappeared, although Breadàlbane represents its synonym—*braghad Alban*, the breast or upland of Alban.

The third case is still more remarkable. Here a scribe mistook *u* for *ri*. This was the more pardonable because, until the eleventh century, it was not customary to dot the *i*. The Western Islands of Scotland were written by Ptolemy *Ebudæ*, and by Pliny *Hæbudæ*. The latter name appears as *Hebrides* in a manuscript from which the early edition of Pliny's 'Natural History' was printed. In that form it took root with us, and was carried by Captain Cook to the southern hemisphere, where he applied it to another group of islands, the New Hebrides.

In the name Ebudæ we seem to have an echo of pre-Celtic or Iverian speech, and the name Bute, or, more correctly, Boot, appears to be the same word.

If these gross blunders have been suffered to corrupt three of the best-known names in Scotland, how many may be as yet undetected among names of lesser note.

LECTURE III.

THE LANGUAGES OF SCOTTISH PLACE-NAMES.

PICTISH SPEECH—CONFLICT OF AUTHORITIES—PLACE-NAMES IN PICTLAND—MYTHICAL DESCENT OF THE PICTS—COLUMBA'S MISSION TO PICTLAND—PICTISH VOCABLES—POLYGLOT PASSAGE IN BEDE'S CHRONICLE—THE PLACE-NAMES OF GALLOWAY—CONCLUSIONS—ANGLO-SAXON SPEECH—THE FRISIAN COLONIES—ORDER OF GENERIC AND SPECIFIC IN TEUTONIC COMPOUNDS—CORRUPT FORMS.

Pictish.

IN the first two lectures of this course we have considered the evidence of a pre-Celtic, presumably non-Aryan, speech, and examined the characteristics of Celtic, in its two branches of Gaelic and Welsh, and we have now to encounter the problem presented by the language of the Picts.

When the Dalriadic colony of Irish-Scots settled in Cowal, Lorn, Kintyre, Isla, and Jura at the close of the fifth century, the greater part of Alban or Caledonia was in possession of a people known as Cruithni or Picts, and it need hardly be said how much difference of opinion prevails at this day as to the ethnographic affinity of the Picts.

Their Languages. 55

Mr Whitley Stokes has given the latest summary of the situation in regard to this people as follows :—

As to the linguistic and ethnological affinities of the Picts, four irreconcilable hypotheses have been formed. The first, due to Pinkerton, is that the Picts were Teutons, and spoke a Gothic dialect. No one now believes in this. The second, started by Professor Rhys, is that the Picts were non-Aryans, whose language was overlaid by loans from Welsh and Irish ; the third, the property of Mr Skene, is that they were Celts, but Gaelic Celts rather than Cymric ; the fourth, and, in my judgment, the true hypothesis, favoured by Professor Windisch and Mr A. Macbain, is that they were Celts, but more nearly allied to the Cymry than to the Gael.[1]

This problem concerns our present purpose in so far, that part of that purpose is to classify Scottish place-names under the languages of the various races which at one time or other dwelt in our land. We must start upon the inquiry into the Pictish nomenclature without any preconceived idea—without any leaning to the theory of Mr Skene that the Picts were Gaelic Celts, or to that of Mr Whitley Stokes that they were Welsh Celts, or to that of Professor Rhys that they were not Celts at all, but Iverians or Firbolg, whose language became infused with Gaelic and Welsh vocables.

We have neither living speech nor, practically, any Pictish literature to guide us. Of the Pictish Chronicle there are two editions, one in Latin, sup-

[1] Beiträge zur kunde der indogermanischen sprachen, 1892.

posed to be a translation of the Gaelic or Pictish original; the other in Gaelic of the Irish Nennius, which Mr Skene held to have been compiled by the monks of Brechin in the tenth century.

The marginal entries in the 'Book of Deer' are in the Aberdeenshire vernacular of the eleventh and twelfth centuries, and are the Gaelic of Alban,—the Latin text of the Gospels themselves being, probably, a couple of hundred years older.

These two are positively the only manuscripts which we can identify as having been produced in Pictland, or, for the matter of that, in the whole of Alban, and they are in ordinary Alban Gaelic.

<small>Place-names in Pictland.</small>   There remains, therefore, to us as our only resource the expedient of closely examining the place-names in those districts forming the ancient Cruithentuath, or land of the Picts, and noting such peculiarities as distinguish them from those in other parts of Scotland.

It is well known that by Pictish law succession was reckoned, not through the father but through the mother. Hence in the ninth century Kenneth, the son of Alpin, king of the Dalriadic Scots by a Pictish mother, succeeded his father as king of the Scots, and through his mother inherited the throne of the Picts. The united kingdom became known as Scotia or Scotland, and henceforward the old name of the northern half of this island, Alba, was heard no more until the dukedom of Albany—that is, Albannach, the people of Alban—was conferred, in a solemn council held at Scone, on 28th April 1398, upon Robert, third son of Robert II. It is strange to reflect that perhaps the best-known locality which now bears this ancient place-name is a street running into Piccadilly, though the Highlanders still talk of the natives of Scotland as Albannach, to distinguish them from Saisneach, or Englishmen. The name Alban is really the genitive case of Alba, the old name of Pictland, just as Erin is the genitive of Eire, the land of the Ernai.

The Picts who were thus superseded by the Scots in the monarchy and the name of their land are stated in the Pictish Chronicle to be descended, like the Scots, from the Scythians, who were called Albani, from their fair hair. Obviously this is only a strained attempt to account for the name, but I wish to draw your attention to the hint at ethnography here. If the Picts, as Professor Rhys would have us believe, were non-Aryan—that is, in no way akin to the Celts—it is *not* probable that the Pictish chronicler would claim for them a common origin with the Dalriadic Gael. *Mythical descent of the Picts.*

It is necessary to allude here to a celebrated quatrain occurring in Nennius' edition of the Pictish Chronicle, because great, and, as it seems to me, undue stress has been laid upon it by ethnologists and philologers.

The Chronicle states that Cruidne, the son of

Cinge, was the father of the Picts or Cruidne in this island. The lines then run:—

> "Seven sons there were to Cruidne,
> Seven parts they made of Alban;
> Cait, Ce, Cerig, warlike men,
> Fib, Fidach, Fotla, Fortrenn."

Now, five of these names are still attached to districts in old Pictland.

Caithness is *Cait*, with the suffix of the Norse *nes*, a promontory.

Cirig is pretty well hidden in Mearns, but easily traced in the original form *Maghgirginn*, or the plain of Cirig.

Fib has become Fife.

Fotla has become Athole, formerly *Ath foitle* or *Ath fotla*.

And *Fortrenn* is the district, including Strathearn, between Forth and Tay.

Professor Rhys hazards the identity o Fidach with Glen Fiddich in Banff, and elsewhere he traces a resemblance to it in Galweidia, Gallovidia, Galloway; but in both instances, I submit, he has nothing to go on but pure conjecture, and in the latter sets aside the easy and pretty obvious explanation given by Mr Skene.

This would leave Moray and Ross to be placed under the second son, Ce.

Now, I am bound to say I regard this explanation of these names with the utmost suspicion. It is so like an instance of the inveterate habit of Celtic bards of explaining place-names by the creation of imaginary heroes. One of these seven names, Fodla, has already served, it will be remembered, as one of the poetic names of Ireland, which, with Eire and Banba, are said in the 'Leabhar Gabhala' to be derived from the wives of the three rulers at the time of the Milesian conquest. In that case there can be little doubt that the bards fitted ready-made princesses to the names which they found attached to the provinces,—just as Nennius, in his account of the Milesian invasion, accounts for the Scuithe or Scots as descendants of Scotta, daughter of the Pharaoh who perished in the Red Sea.

It is with great diffidence that I venture to hesitate in founding upon what has been accepted by very high authorities as the derivation of Caithness, Mearns, Fife, Athole, and Fortrenn. The probability seems to me to be that these eponymous heroes were created to account for the names already in use, rather than that the names were conferred in commemoration of the sons of Cruidne.

Those who hold that the Picts were of pre-Celtic race, distinct in origin and speech from the Gael, have to admit that before the sixth century they had adopted the Gaelic language. Adamnan, describing the mission of St Columba to the Pictish King Brude, suggests no difficulty in his intercourse with that ruler nor with the Druid Broichan, and he mentions only two occasions when the services of an interpreter were required. The first was when <sidenote>Columba's mission to Pictland.</sidenote>

Artbrannan, the aged chief of the "Geonian cohort," came by sea to meet him in the isle of Skye. It is pretty clear that the men of Skye spoke Gaelic, for Adamnan goes on to say that they named the spring where Artbrannan was baptised *Dobur Artbrannan*,—*dobur* being the old word in Gaelic for "water," the same as *tiobar*, a well, which occurs in place-names all over Scotland as Tibber, Chipper, and Kibbert.

The second instance of the use of an interpreter was when Columba converted an old peasant and his family. These persons, probably from remote parts of the Pictish province, might be Iverians or Firbolg, speaking the old language, or if Picts, using a local dialect.

The use of an interpreter does not necessarily imply conference between two persons speaking a different language. John of Trevisa, a Cornishman, writing English in 1357, says: "All the language of the Northumbrians, and especially at York, is so sharp, slitting, grating, and unshapen, that we Southerners can scarcely understand that language." Indeed it may be doubted if a Cornishman of the present day could dispense with an interpreter for occasional use, if he were set down in a northern English county. St Columba, speaking pure Gaelic of the north of Ireland, might easily be puzzled by the speech of some of the natives in Pictland.

Last year I was chairman of a departmental Committee appointed to inquire into the plague of voles in the Border counties. An interpreter became necessary to explain to an English member of the Committee the language of an Ettrick shepherd, who, speaking of the mischievous habits of the carrion-crow, said, "The corbies is vara guilty for pykin' the een oot o' a yow, an' her leevin';"[1] which also rather puzzled the shorthand writer.

But there is another passage in John of Trevisa's translation of Higden's 'Polycronicon' which seems to have an important bearing on the relation of Pictish to Gaelic. In describing the various races and languages of Great Britain, he says: "Welshmen and Scots that be not mixed with other nations preserve wellnigh their first language and speech, except that the Scots, that were some time confederate and dwelt with the Picts, draw somewhat after their speech." This is the reverse of the process which Professor Rhys imagines to have taken place, when, after stating in the Rhind lectures five years ago that "the Picts, whatever they were, were no Celts, . . . [but] a race which, however brave and hardy, cannot be called Aryan," he went on to explain the prevalence of Gaelic names in Pictland by assuming that the Pictish language had been largely altered and added to from Gaelic.

Examination of the place-names in the territory of the Northern Picts, north of the Forth and Clyde, reveals certain vocables used as generic terms which are not to be found elsewhere in Scotland. It is

<small>Pictish vocables.</small>

---

[1] Picking out the eyes of a ewe while she is still alive.

not unreasonable to look upon these as Pictish. Mr Skene enumerated four of these occurring commonly as prefixes — namely, Pit, For, Fin, and Auchter. *Pit* is written *Pette* in the 'Book of Deer,' where its meaning is perfectly clear as the equivalent of the Gaelic *baile*, a portion of land, a farm or townland. In fact, Dr John Stuart supplied instances of the synonymous and indiscriminate use of *pit* and *bal* at the present day in the following Forfarshire names:—

Pitmachie	. . .	Balmachie.
Pitskelly	. . .	Balskelly.
Pitargus	. . .	Balargus.
Pitruchie	. . .	Balruchie.
Pitkeerie	. . .	Balkeerie.
Pitglasso	. . .	Balglasso.

Pitfoùr and Balfoùr are different places bearing synonymous names — *pett* and *baile fuar*, the cold croft, or croft of the spring well. In Perthshire, Pitagòwan, near Blair Atholl, is identical in meaning with Balgòwn in Wigtownshire—*pett a' gobhain, baile gobhain,* the smith's croft.

But there is another Gaelic word used instead of *baile*, which is even nearer to *pett*. *Both*, a dwelling, a booth, is a term occurring in many languages, from the Aryan root *bhu*, to be, to grow, to dwell, to build; whence the Sanskrit *bhavana*, a house, a place to be in, from *bhu*, to be. The Anglo-Saxon *botl*, a house, which gives us Nèwbattle in Mid-Lothian, Mòrebattle in Roxburghshire, Buittle in Kirkcudbright, and Bootle in Lancashire, is a cog-

Their Languages. 63

nate word. So is the Norse *bo, by,* forming the suffix in Lòckerbie, Cànonbie, &c. It is not unlikely that *pit* or *pett* was the Pictish form of the Gaelic *bod* or *both.*

In the land-names of the Isle of Bute there has been preserved a form intermediate between Gaelic *both* and Pictish *pett,* which appears as the prefix *butt,* in names like Buttanlòin—*butt an loin,* the marsh croft; Buttcùrry—*butt curaich,* the moor or marsh croft; Buttdùbh, the black croft; Buttnacòille, the wood croft; Buttnacrèig, the crag croft; Buttnamàdda—*butt nam madadh* (madduh), croft of the wolves or dogs.

The old name of Provanhall, near Shettleston, was Barlannar or Buthlornoc. In Prince David's Inquisition this is written Pathelenerke, showing that Pette or Pathe was interchangeable with Both or Buth. Again, Pitgòwnie, near Elgin, used to be Bothgouanan; and Pitfòddles, near Aberdeen, was Badfodullis. Then in Perthshire, while Pitcastle occurs near Pitlochrie and again near Ballinluig—*pett caiseail,* castle-croft—near Callander it turns up as Bochastle—*both chaisteail.*

Now we know that *p* was an objectionable consonant to Gaelic pronunciation, and when ordinary Gaelic came to be spoken throughout the territory of the Picts, the Gael would have to encounter the difficulty of this consonant occurring in Pictish place-names. The easiest way to get over the difficulty would be to soften the *p* by aspiration into *f.*

I have mentioned that Mr Skene referred to *For* and *Fin* as prefixes characteristic of Pictish place-names. There is some probability that in these syllables we have the Pictish *pett* or *pit* retranslated into Gaelic.

The full form of *For* is *Fothur*, as in Fothuirtabhaicht, now Forteviot; Fothurdun, now Fordun. Other examples are Fothringham, Fortrose, Fortingall, Fettercairn, Fetteresso, and Fetternear. The full form of *Fin* is *Fothen*, as Fothenaven, now Finhaven. Take one of the Pictish place-names in the 'Book of Deer,' Pette an Muilenn, the mill-croft (now Pitmellan, near Newburgh), apply the aspirate, and it becomes Fethenmuilenn or Finmullin. Subject Fothenaven (Finhaven) to the converse process, and it becomes *Pett an amhuinn*, the river-croft. Similarly Fettercàirn in Forfarshire is the aspirated form of Pitcàirn in Perthshire, the *n* changing easily into *r*, as we have seen *cnoc* changes into *crochd*; and the name of Ninian is often altered into Ringan in Galloway.

If this be so, then *Fin* and *For*, which Mr Skene relied on as Pictish prefixes, turn out to be no more than *Fothen* and *Fothir*—that is, *Pit* or *Pett* followed by the article; and *Pit* itself to be a local or tribal pronunciation of the Gaelic *both*, Welsh *bwth*. Three out of four of his test Pictish syllables prove to be different stages of the same word. It is the more remarkable that the kinship of *pett* to *feth* or *foth* did not occur to Mr Skene, because in analysing the to-names of the thirty Brudes, kings of the Picts, when he comes to Brude Feth he says, "*feth* seems the same as *pet.*"

Notwithstanding the partial change of the Pictish *pit* under Gaelic influence to *fin* and *for*, it still remains the commoner form of the prefix in ancient Pictland. The County Directory of Scotland contains 140 place-names in that district beginning with *Pet* or *Pit*.

There remains Mr Skene's fourth Pictish prefix to be dealt with—*Auchter;* but this is not, as he supposed, confined to the territory of the Northern Picts. It is, as he says, the Gaelic *uachdar*, upper land, and occurs in Ireland as Oughteràrd in Galway—*uachdar ard*, the high upland—and Oughterànny in Kildare—*uachdar raithneach*, ferny upland. Moreover, it is not uncommon in Galloway, which, though an old Pictish district, exhibits few Pictish peculiarities in its Gaelic nomenclature. In Leswalt parish there is Ochteralìnachan—*uachdarach lìnachan*, upland of the flax-field; in Inch parish Ochtralùre—*uachdarach lobhair*, the leper's upland; in Kirkmabreck parish, Auchtrievàne—*uachdarach bhán*, white upland; in Portpatrick parish, Ochtrimakàin—M'Kean's upland.

The most direct piece of information afforded us about a Pictish place-name is supplied by Bede, who, writing in the eighth century, says that the Wall of Antonine began about two miles west of Abercorn, "at a place called in the language of the Picts Peanfahel, but in that of the Angles Penneltun." *Polyglot passage in Bede's Chronicle.*

Nennius says that the wall was called in Welsh Guaul, and reached from Penguaul, "which town is called Cenail in Gaelic (*Scoticè*), but in English Peneltun." This Peneltun is the Celtic Pen-guaul, wall-head or wall's end, with the characteristic Anglian suffix, *tún*. The prefix *pen* has dropped off in use, and the name now remains as Walton, three miles west of Abercorn, while the name Cenail has moved some three miles further west to Kinnèil.

Thus we have the name of a single place in four different dialects :—

Gaelic . . .	Cenail.
Welsh . . .	Penguaul.
Pictish . . .	Peanfahel.
Old Northern English .	Peneltun.

From this it would appear that the Pictish equivalent to the Welsh *gu* before a vowel, tending to sound *w* or *hw*, was *f*. Further confirmation of this is contained in a statement of Reginald of Durham, who, speaking of a Pictish scholar at Kirkcudbright (*scolasticus Pictorum apud Cuthbrictis chirch*), says that the clergy of that church were known in the language of the Picts as *scollofthes*. Here again the Pictish substitute *f* for the guttural, for the Welsh word is *ysgolhaig* and the Gaelic *sgolog*.

To the same influence may be traced the name Futerna appearing in some of the Irish writings for Whithorn — a phonetic rendering of the Pictish pronunciation of the Anglo-Saxon *hwit ærn*, white house.

Their Languages. 67

With regard to the people of Galloway, who were recognised as Picts so late as the Battle of the Standard in the twelfth century, it must be observed that although exposed to Welsh influence along the frontier of Strathclyde, from Loch Ryan to the Nith, little if any Welsh element can be traced in their names. Their territory was marked off by a rampart sixty miles long, which, known as the Deil's Dyke, may still be traced across the hills from Lefnòl on Loch Ryan to the Nith opposite Carronbridge. Settlements of Welsh families within that territory were exceptional, and, as has been already observed, are recorded as foreign in Gaelic place-names like Culbràtten and Drumbrèddan. As a whole, the Celtic place-names of Galloway are cast in the same mould as those of Ulster, and lead to the conclusion that, whatever dialect they spoke at first, these Niduarian Picts, or Picts beyond the Nith, used for many centuries a language not greatly differing from that of Ulster, Man, and Scottish Dalriada.

Place-names of Galloway.

Taking, then, the consonant f as a favourite Pictish lip-sound, it affords a very uncertain test in the place-names of Pictish territory. It may represent one of four things—

1st. A Pictish substitute for the sound gu or w in Welsh, as Peanfahel for Penguaul, or for hw in Anglo-Saxon, as Futerna for Whithorn.

2d. The reduction of the Pictish p to an aspirated labial, when Gaelic overflowed the Pictish dialect, as Fothenaven or Finhaven for Pett-an-amhuinn.

3d. The aspiration of *p* in a Gaelic vocable such as *pol*, water, as in Falnure, which in old maps is sometimes written for Palnùre, a stream in Kirkcudbrightshire—*pol na' iubhar*, stream of the yews; or Falbàe, an alternative form for Polbàe—*pol beith*, stream of the birches.

4th. Lastly, it may be a Gaelic sound unaltered, as Fìntray—*fionn traigh*, white strand; and even that is often rendered by *gu* in Welsh, as *gwyn* for *fionn*, the Gaelic Lumphànan or Kilfìnnan becoming Kilwìnning in Strathclyde, or Kirkgunzeon in Eastern Galloway. On the other hand, the *f* (with the value of *v*) is preserved in some Welsh names, like Llanfìnan in Anglesea.

<small>In Scotland, Gaelic survived Pictish and Welsh.</small>

One thing alone seems tolerably certain, that in certain districts of Southern Scotland Pictish and Welsh alike died out before Gaelic, and Professor Rhys attributes the general uniformity of the Lowland Scottish dialect to the fact that the Anglo-Saxon had in those districts only one language to encounter in the struggle for the vernacular. But he traces another influence in the peculiarities of Aberdeenshire Scottish. He points to the persistence with which the natives of that part of Scotland substitute *f* for *wh* as evidence that in the north-east Anglo-Saxon came in contact with Pictish speech. So when an Aberdonian says, "Fa fuppit the fite fulpie!" where a Dumfries man would say,

"Wha whuppit the white whelpie!" he is acting under the same linguistic necessity which made the Pict of Manann talk of Peanfahel, instead of Penguaul or Cenail. And just as the Pict said *pett* instead of *both* or *bad*, so the Aberdonian prefers narrow vowel sounds to broad, and says "dee" and "min" for "do" and "moon."

After all, it seems to me, after a very careful examination of place-names in Pictish districts, that there is nothing to carry us beyond the conclusion to which Mr Skene, with extraordinary diligence and acumen, brought himself thirty years ago, and I cannot do better than repeat it in his own words :— <small>Conclusion.</small>

I consider, therefore, that Pictish was a low Gaelic dialect; and following out the analogy, the result I come to is this, that Cymric and Gaelic had each a high and low variety; that Cornish and Breton were high Cymric dialects, Welsh low Cymric; that old Scottish, spoken by the Scotti, now represented by Irish, Scotch Gaelic, and Manx, was the high Gaelic dialect. . . . In the north of Ireland and the west of Scotland the Picts must, at an early period, have become blended with the Scots, and their form of Gaelic assimilated to the Scottish.

It is, perhaps, disappointing not to come to a more definite explanation of that which Bede spoke of as one of the four languages of Britain; but I submit that the evidence will support no other hypothesis, and though many students have not shrunk from bolder speculation as to the language of the Picts, it does not seem to be consistent with scientific caution.

Anglo-Saxon speech. Next in order of antiquity to place-names in the various dialects of Celtic must be reckoned those in the Teutonic group, which, for convenience, we may class as Anglo-Saxon.

The Frisian colonies. It is usually assumed, on the authority of Bede, that the Saxon colonies in Great Britain began during the fifth century; for that chronicler, writing in the beginning of the eighth century, fixes A.D. 449 as the date of their first arrival: but it is certain that there were earlier settlements than that. Prosper, writing in 455, states in his Chronicle, under the year 441, " Britain up to this time is brought *widely* under dominion of the Saxons by various conflicts and transactions."

It is true that the Angles first settled under Ida in Northumberland in 547, but Mr Skene collected evidence of descents and settlements made long before that date by the Frisii or Frisones, a Teutonic people inhabiting the country between the Rhine and the Ems. He thinks they are the people known to the Gaels as Comgalls, just as the Norse became known as Fingalls, or fair-skinned foreigners, and the Danes as Dubhgalls, or dark foreigners; and he identifies their settlement with a place on the northern shore of the Firth of Forth, between the Ochils and the sea, which Angus the Culdee, writing in the ninth century, calls the Comgalls. This name is quoted in the Old Statistical Account of

Inverkeillour, where the old name of the parish is given as Conghoilles.

In Congalton, near North Berwick, Mr Skene again recognised the name of these foreigners, for although the name has a very Anglian appearance, yet in an old charter of this barony one of the boundary marks is defined as Knockin gallstane— that is, *cnoc Comgall*, the Comgalls' hill, with the Anglian *tun* or *stan* as suffix. Further, in the Irish Annals, under the years 711, 712, and 730, there are notices of slaughter of the race of Comgall, at a place called Tarbet Boitter. Now the isle of Fìdra or Fètheray, about three miles west of North Berwick, contains an isthmus, above which there is a rocky height called the Castle of Tàrbet. Tarbet is the common Gaelic term for an isthmus, from *tarruin bád*, draw-boat, a place where boats are drawn overland, to avoid rough seas at the cape. The modern name Fetheray or Fidra is probably the same as Boitter of the annalist, the initial *b* taking the aspirate, and the Norse *ey*, an island, added.

In a royal charter of 1509, conveying this island to Henry Congalton, it is described as *insulam et terras de Fetheray unacum monte Castri earundem vocat. Tarbet;* but in the chartulary of Dryburgh Abbey as *insula de Elboitel*. Elboitel is written in Pont's map Old Battel, which simply means old house, A.S. *eld botl*.

To a third locality identified with these settlers they have left attached, not the name of Comgall, by which they were known to the Gaels, but their own name of Frisii. Of the twenty-eight cities named by Nennius in Britain, one is Caer Bretain, the fortress of the Britons—Dumbarton; another Caer Pheris, which is probably the fortress of the Frisians—Dumfries.

William of Malmesbury, describing the discovery of the sepulchre of Walwin, nephew of King Arthur, in 1087, says, "He reigned a most renowned knight in that part of Britain which is still named Walweithia, but was driven from his kingdom by the brother and nephew of Hengist." Now we know better than to follow this writer in his suggestion that Galloway, which he writes Walweithia, was named after Walwin; but this brother and nephew of Hengist were no other than Octa and Ebissa, who, as Nennius informs us, came with forty cyuls, sailed round the land of the Picts, devastated Orkney, and occupied several districts beyond the Frisian sea (*ultra mare Fresicum*). Walweithia is another form of Galwyddel, the Welsh name for Galloway, whence the inference is clear that the Frisians made a settlement in that province, and ruled it from Dumfries.

This may have originated the name Galwyddel, Galgaidhel, or Galloway, meaning the foreign Gael, or Gaels under foreign rule; and the subsequent subjection of Galloway to the Anglian kingdom of Northumberland, of which it formed a part for many centuries, difficult to account for on geographical grounds, and the establishment of an Anglian bishopric at *Candida Casa* or Whithorn, may both have arisen from the early subjection of the province to Frisian rovers.

I do not forget that, in expressing the opinion that Frisians were among the earliest Teutonic colonists of North Britain, I find myself at variance with so high an authority on Anglian dialects as Professor Skeat, who holds, in his volumes on the 'Principles of English Etymology,' that this people were spread over the middle and southern districts of England, rather than the northern parts of the island; but it would be difficult to account for Nennius speaking of the Firth of Forth as *Mare Fresicum*, except by the fact that Frisians had settled on the shores of it. Josceline also, in his 'Life of Kentigern,' refers to Culross as *litus Fresicum*, the Frisian coast.

Howbeit, the question as to which of the Germanic tribes first settled in Scotland can receive little light from the form of place-names; for the old Frisian language was very nearly allied to Anglo-Saxon, and it would be impossible at this time to distinguish between names conferred by Frisians, and those by Angles, Saxons, or Jutes. What does concern the present inquiry is that some of the Teutonic place-names in Scotland, originating in early Frisian settlements, may be of higher antiquity than those dating from the later invasions of Angles and Saxons.

74 Scottish Land-Names.

Order of generic and specific syllables.

One broad distinction separates Germanic compound names from Celtic. In the latter, as has been shown, the generic term *generally* precedes the specific; in Germanic or Anglian compounds, the specific term *invariably* precedes the generic. The stress faithfully follows the specific syllable, hence in Anglian place-names the stress most often lies on the first syllable, in Celtic most often on the ultimate or penultimate.

Corrupt forms.

Frisians, Angles, Saxons, and Jutes, however little lettered their colonists may have been, spoke dialects of a literary language, and their vocables are easily interpreted by comparison with Anglo-Saxon and Old Northern English. Nevertheless, one has to be on his guard against the tricks which modern topographers are so prone to play with names of which the meaning is not at once apparent.

We have seen how the Welsh *llanerch* became Lànrig and then Lòngridge; Stòneykirk, a parish in Wigtownshire, has been made absurd by a similar process. This name is written phonetically in the Register of the Great Seal in 1535, Steneker; in 1546, Stenakere; and in 1559, Stennaker. Thus far early spellings mislead rather than assist us; but as late as 1725 it appears in the papers of the Court of Session as Stevenskirk. It is a dedication to St Stephen; the popular contraction "Steenie" sounded like "stany," and would-be-genteel scribes wrote it "stoney," though the name has no more to do with stones than it has with gooseberry-bushes. The local pronunciation is Staneykirk.

Not seldom the Anglo-Saxon *circ* was borrowed in Gaelic districts for use in a Gaelic compound name, as Kirkcùdbright—*circ Cudbricht*, Cuthbert's church; Kirkgùnzeon — *circ Guinnin*, St Finan's church, which you find with full Gaelic expression at Kilwinning in Ayrshire. A.S. *circ* becomes Gaelic loan-word.

These bilingual names are but a reflection of the social state of the country, when different races and languages were contesting for the mastery. In a charter printed in Anderson's 'Diplomata Scotiæ,' it is set forth how Richard de Morville, Constable of Scotland in 1166, sells Edmund, the son of Bonda, and Gillemichel his brother, to Henry St Clair. Here Edmund and Bonda are Saxon names, but Gillemichel is Gaelic, "Michael's servant."

Kirk as a suffix may sometimes be confused with the Gaelic *coirce* or *coirc* (kyorky or kyork), oats. Thus Barnkìrk in Wigtownshire is the contracted form of Barnkìrky in Kirkcudbright; both signify *barr an coirce*, oats-hill. But the local application of the stress is a sure indication of the specific syllable.

LECTURE IV.

THE LANGUAGES OF SCOTTISH PLACE-NAMES.

SCANDINAVIAN OR OLD NORSE AND DANISH — OBLITERATION OF CELTIC SPEECH IN THE NORTHERN ISLES—MIXTURE OF TONGUES IN THE WESTERN ISLES—NORSE NAMES DISGUISED AS GAELIC—ASPIRATION OF GAELIC CONSONANTS—CONFUSION ON THE MAPS—GAELIC NAMES DISGUISED AS NORSE—RELATIVE ANTIQUITY OF CERTAIN PLACE-NAMES—TRACES OF NORSE OCCUPATION IN SCOTLAND—RESEMBLANCE BETWEEN NORSE AND SAXON SPEECH—NORSE TEST-WORDS—THEIR DISTRIBUTION—INFERENCES THEREFROM—MIXTURE OF LANGUAGES IN STRATHCLYDE—THE GAELIC *DAL* AND NORSE *DALR*—DIFFERENCE IN THEIR MEANING—NORSE AND SAXON LOAN-WORDS IN ENGLISH.

Scandinavian or Norse and Danish.

N the eighth and ninth centuries an important addition was made to the ethnology of Alban by the incursion and settlement of predatory bands of Norwegians and Danes, resulting in the establishment of many Scandinavian place-names in our islands. The wealth which some of the monasteries had by this time accumulated from the offerings of the pious was the lure for these marauders, and the first of a long series of depredations is thus

Their Languages. 77

described by Simeon of Durham as taking place on the monastic house of Lindisfarne in 793 :—

The Pagans from the northern region came with armed ships to Britain like stinging hornets, and overran the country in all directions like fierce wolves, plundering, tearing, and killing not only sheep and oxen, but priests and levites, and choirs of monks and nuns. They came to the church of Lindisfarne and laid all waste with dreadful havoc, trod with unhallowed feet the holy altars, and carried off all the treasures of the holy church. Some of the brethren they killed, some they carried off in chains, many they cast out naked and loaded with insults, some they drowned in the sea.

Next year, 794, they attacked the Hebrides. These islands they called the Sudreyar or Southern Isles, to distinguish them from the Nodreyar or Northern Isles of Orkney and Shetland; and it is a curious instance of the conservative element in place-names that, although of course the Sudreyar or Hebrides are not now within the diocese of Man, the official title of that see is still "Sodor and Man."

The people of Orkney and Shetland once, it may be assumed, spoke Iverian, Gaelic, or Pictish, for the early Ogham inscriptions in Shetland have been interpreted in a Goidhelic dialect; but little trace of these tongues can now be detected in their place-names, which are almost exclusively Norse or later English. To this the first syllable of the name Orkney affords an important exception. Diodorus Siculus, writing in A.D. 57, mentions Orcas as one of the extremities of Britain. *Orc*, in Gaelic, means

^{Native speech obliterated in the Northern Isles.}

a large beast, especially a whale: when the Norsemen took possession they may have found them called Whale Islands, and adding their own *ey*, island, to the native name, called them Orkney, just as we saw in the last lecture that Boitter or Fether in the Forth became Fètheray or Fìdra. Of course, when we speak of the Orkney Islands we are guilty of a pleonasm. It is as if we said "Whale Isle Islands."[1]

St Ninian visited them in the fifth century, and left his name attached to North Rònaldshay, so spelt from false analogy with South Rònaldshay. This is an instance of the paramount necessity of obtaining the earliest written form of a name, for North Rònaldshay is written in the Sagas Rinansey —that is, Ringan's Isle—Ringan being a common alternative form of Ninian; whereas South Ronaldshay is Rögnvals-ey—Ronald's Isle.

Sir Robert Sibbald, in 1711, stated that the inhabitants of Orkney and Shetland still spoke the "Gothick or Norwegian language, which they call Norn, now much worn out," among themselves, though able to speak English to strangers. Hence we see that not only has all trace of the original native speech been obliterated by the long occupation of the Norsemen, but there has not been in Orkney and Shetland a regurgitation of the Gaelic

[1] The hamlet of Aith, near Conningsburgh, seems to be mentioned in the Ogham inscription found at the latter place; which has been interpreted *ehte con mor*—that is, the *ait*, or house-site, of great Conn.

language, such as took place in the Hebrides and in Strathclyde. These islands form, I believe, a unique instance of the suppression within historic time by a conquering race, not only of the spoken language of the conquered people—that is common enough—but of the names attached to places in that language. Hence it follows that almost every place-name in Orkney and Shetland may be pronounced with confidence to be not more than 1000, or at most 1100, years old.

All the names in Orkney and Shetland which are not English are in Old Norse, a dialect which has been preserved to our days in the native literature of Iceland, of which country it also remains, with very little change, the spoken language. It is, therefore, as easy for an Icelandic scholar to read the meaning of place-names in Orkney and Shetland, as for an Englishman to interpret those in Warwickshire. Much more so, indeed, for there are Celtic names in the Midlands, such as Avon and Leam, and Norse names, like Rugby and Heythrop; and besides, modern Icelandic is much nearer Old Norse than literary English is to Old Mercian or Anglo-Saxon.

But the task is not so simple when we come to deal with the Western Isles. The Norse rule did not endure so long there as in Orkney, and when it was withdrawn, Gaelic, which probably had never entirely died out, reasserted itself. There are plenty of Norse names in the Hebrides, but some of these

Mixture of tongues in the Western Isles.

have undergone strange metamorphoses in the process of transcription under the rules of Gaelic orthography.

Effect of aspiration.
In order to explain the form which some Norse names have assumed under Gaelic influence, it is necessary to enter somewhat minutely into an examination of the so-called aspiration of consonants in Gaelic. The consonants *b, c, d, f, g, m, p, s, t* are all liable to it. In the Irish alphabet aspiration is indicated by a dot over the character; thus *b* aspirated is written *ḃ*. But the Scottish Gael never had an alphabet, and when his language came to be written, he borrowed the character *h* and wrote *bh*.[1] The term "aspiration" is strained by Irish and Gaelic grammarians far beyond what English linguists understand it to mean. Aspiration properly means the introduction of the aspirate, so as to alter the sound of a consonant into another sound made by the same organ. Thus *p* aspirated becomes *ph* or *f*, both being labial sounds. But in Gaelic the mere slurring or dropping of a consonant is dignified by the name of aspiration. Falkirk is locally pronounced Fàhkirk, but we do not consider that in this Anglian name the *l* has been aspirated; it is simply not sounded, because the meaning of the speaker is

[1] "Haliday," says O'Donovan, "classes *l* among the aspirable consonants, and marks it, when aspirated, with two dots, thus *l̈*. And it is true that, when coming after all those particles which cause other consonants to be aspirated, it has, in some parts of Ireland, a different sound from the primitive one."—('Irish Grammar,' p. 32.) No doubt the Welsh aspirate the consonant *l*, which is then written *ll*, as in *llan*, pronounced *hlān*.

perfectly clear without the effort of sounding the *l*. So an Englishman does not now trill the *r* in "church," "part," "master," or "servant"; he slurs it to save himself trouble: but Gaelic grammarians are pedantic sticklers for orthography, and insist that consonants are silenced, not for the convenience or from the laziness of the speaker, but because they are aspirated.

Now of the Gaelic consonants *b, c, g, m*, and *p* may be properly considered as subject to aspiration.

B and *m* with the aspirate become *v* or *w*, and in the latter state are liable to cease to sound altogether. *C* becomes a strong guttural, as in the word *loch*; *g* a weak one, like our *h*; and *p* becomes *f* as in English. But the remaining consonants classed as being subject to the aspirate—*d, f, s,* and *t*—are in reality only subject to slur, though in this condition they are elaborately written:—

Irish . . .	ḋ ḟ ṡ ṫ
Scottish Gaelic .	dh fh sh th

They retain, at most, but a faint sound of *h*, and would be more correctly represented in writing by an apostrophe.

Nevertheless, not content with insisting on writing organic consonants which had become silent, Irish scribes loved to load their manuscripts with voiceless consonants forming no part of the original word. Norsemen called Olaf have left their name attached to both places and persons in Ireland and Scotland. In order to represent the sound of this name, Irish writers took the roundabout way of spelling it *Amhalghadh* or *Amhlaiph*, to represent the sound Owlhay. Macheràlly and Teràlly, in the parish of Kirkmaiden, Wigtownshire, might have baffled the etymologist, but for the means of comparing them with Magherally and Tirawley in Ireland, the latter of which is written *tír Amhalghaidh* or *Amhalghadha* in the Irish Annals. The old pronunciation is preserved in Wigtownshire—Macherowlay. As a personal name Olaf is familiar to us in the Gaelic patronymic, Macaulay; but it is very fully disguised in Ullapool, which is the Norse Olabol, *Olafr bólstaðr* or homestead, and in the Gaelic Baile-Uilph, in Islay, meaning the same thing.

Norse names in Gaelic guise.

This highly artificial system of orthography has had a curious and puzzling effect upon Norse names in Gaelic districts. The Norse *gjá*, a chasm, written phonetically in English "goe," becomes *geodha* in Gaelic with the same sound, and enters commonly into place-names on the coasts of lands formerly held by the Norse. The Gaelic equivalent is *slochd*, as in Slouchnagàrie, on the Wigtownshire coast—*slochd na' caora*, sheep's gulley; but the word *geodha* exists in Gaelic as a loan-word, and forms a common prefix in the Isle of Man, as Giau-ny-kirree, sheep's gulley.

But a still more perplexing effect of the Gaelic aspirate upon Norse names remains to be described. No word can be rightly written in Gaelic beginning with the letter *h*, although nothing is commoner than the aspiration of the initial consonant in the genitive case, as *an coileach,* the cock, *a' choilich,* of the cock; *am fear* (fer), the man, gen. *an fhir* (heer), of the man. Thus Gaelic scribes concluded that all place-names beginning with *h* were in the genitive, and proceeded to construct an imaginary nominative. Hàbost, in Lewis, is the Norse *hallr bólstaðr,* sloping farm, from *hallr,* a word that gives names to places in Orkney called Holland, and in Shetland, Houlland,[1] equivalent to the name Clènerie or Clèndrie, occurring frequently as a land-name, and representing the Gaelic *claenrach,* sloping. Or the name may be derived from *hallr,* a big stone, in which case the Gaelic equivalent of Habost would be Balnacloich. But the meaning of Habost was unknown to the Gael; so, believing it to be a genitive Thaboist (which to him would have the same sound as Habost), he actually invented a nominative Tàbost to account for the initial aspirate, and that is the name of the place at this day. So Tòrmisdale in Islay has been made the imaginary nominative of Ormisdale, because the Highlanders thought the *t* had been lost by aspiration in the genitive; and Plàdda, the island at the south point of Arran, has for the same reason been substituted for Flad-ey—Flat Island. The name remains unaltered near Oban as Flàdda. On the other hand, the Gaelic phonetic law requires the aspiration of certain consonants in composition, and under its influence the Norse *fjörðr* generally loses

[1] This seems sometimes to mean *haugr land,* island of the howe or hillock.

the initial *f* sound on Gaelic lips: so Sneisfjörðr became Sneisfhord (pronounced Sneezord), now written Snizort; Cnuts-fjörðr became Knòydart, now pronounced, by change of *n* to *r*, Crojarst; but Bròadford in Skye retains the full sound of the Norse *breiðr fjörðr*, broad firth, and there has been as little alteration in Sèaforth.

Confusion on the maps.
All this has led to endless confusion of tongues among the Ordnance surveyors, to whose maps one naturally resorts in studying place-names. In places where Gaelic is still spoken, they have attempted to give some of the Norse names in Gaelic orthography, thereby completely obscuring their etymology. There is, for instance, no *v* in the Gaelic alphabet; in Welsh a single *f* represents *v*, as it does in English "of," *ff* having the value of English *f* in "for." But in Gaelic the sound of *v* must be represented by *bh* or *mh*, so the common Norse word *vík*, a bay, appears on our maps as *bhig*, unless it is Anglicised out of existence, like Bròdick in Arran—*breiðr vík*, broad bay; or, still further disguised in Gaelic, as Sanaigmòre in Islay—*sand vík mór*, great sandy bay. Hèlsvagr is written Loch Thèalasbhaidh (Hellasvah); Hàmnavoe—*höfn vagr*, haven bay, in the northern islands, appears in the southern islands, where Gaelic is spoken, masquerading as Thamnabhaidh.

Sometimes, by an equally misleading process, Norse names receive an English complexion, as Wìndhouse in Shetland, which is really *vind áss*, the windy ridge, equivalent to Barnagèe, in Galloway and elsewhere—the Gaelic *barr na gaoithe* (geuha, gwee).

Yet again, some Gaelic names have lost their Celtic appearance during the long Norse occupation, and have never regained it. Of such is the island of Rum, which is probably all that remains of *I-dhruim*, ridge island, the *d* being silenced by aspiration, just as it has been in Lòrum, in Carlow, all that remains of *leamh-dhruim*, elm ridge, as the name is written in the 'Annals of the Four Masters.'

<small>Gaelic names in Norse guise.</small>

Lèwis, again, is a combination of letters far from Gaelic in appearance, nor does the rendering of it, *I-Liodhus*, in the Sagas, indicate its true origin—in fact, it has suggested the absurd interpretation of the "loud or sounding house," from the noise of the waves. The real meaning is probably that given by Martin in his 'Western Isles'—namely, *leoghas*, marshy land, from *leog*, a marsh.

Many derivations have been given for the name of Uist; but Captain Thomas may be credited with having traced it to its source. *Fearsad* is an old Gaelic word meaning a sand-bar forming a ford; the genitive is *fheirste* (*fh* silent). Such a sand-bar is a well-known feature in the Isle of Uist: the name is *I-fheirste* (eehirst), ford-island, and the *r* dropped out in Scandinavian and English speech, just as it has done in Belfast—*beul-feirste*, ford-mouth. Harris, on the contrary, in spite of its cockney disguise, is a genuine Norse name. It is *hár ey*, high island, correctly describing it as compared with *leoghas*, the marshy northern part of the island. Roderick Macleod signed his name in 1596 as "of the Herrie." The word occurs again in Hàrray, one of the Orkneys.

<small>Relative antiquity of place-names.</small>

It must occur to you, after penetrating thus far into the mystery of names in the Western and Northern Islands, that there is evidence to be gathered of the relative antiquity of some of the place-names. Lewis and Rum existed as names before the arrival of the Norse at the end of the ninth century. Harris and all Norse names, on the other hand, have been conferred subsequently to that date.

<small>Traces of Norse occupation.</small>

Evidence of Norse occupation may be gathered as we travel southwards from the great Scandinavian centre of the Northern and Southern Isles; generally on the sea-coast, as in Ayr—*eyrr*, the beach. Lèndal, near Ballantrae, may be explained as *len dalr*, fief or fee dale; Sìnniness in Wigtownshire as *sunnr nes*, south point; Sènwick in Kirkcudbright, and Sànnox in Arran, as *sand vík*, sandy bay.

But in advancing up the Solway Firth we begin to encounter Scandinavian names far inland, as in the river Æ in Dumfriesshire, and Eye in Berwickshire, both representing the Norse *á*, a river—Lockerbie, Canonbie, &c. These are probably relics of the Norse dominion over Cumberland and Yorkshire, which spread overland from the east coast.

As I have mentioned the characteristic Norse word *eyrr*, a beach, allusion may be made to some peculiar forms it takes. Besides Ayr, the beach, which has given the name to the river, the town, and the county, superseding the old names of Carrick, Kyle, and Cunninghame, there is Air in the Orkneys and Eyri in Iceland; the Point of Ayr in Man, and again at Wirral in Cheshire. The word corresponds to the Gaelic *claddach*, the beach, as Clàdy House and Claddiochdòw in Wigtownshire. The Norsemen called a small island *holmr*, a middle-sized one *ey*, and a large one *land*. *Eyrr land*, beach island, has become Irland in Orkney and Ireland in Shetland.

This, however, has to be remembered, that even with the aid of comparison with modern Icelandic, it must not be assumed too readily that place-names of Scandinavian appearance all originated with Norse occupation. The Angles, though classed as Saxons, came from the district of Angeln in the south of Jutland, and there was probably not a very wide difference between their speech and the Old Danish or Norse; besides which, many Norse vocables found their way into the current speech of the country, where they still remain. *Similarity of Norse and Saxon speech.*

In Norse compound names the specific word precedes the generic, as in other Teutonic languages. Captain Thomas has, however, recorded one exception to this rule in the word *kvi*, a fold or pen, which appears in the Orkneys as Quoyschòrsetter, Quoysmiddie, Quoybanks, Quoy Ronald, as if Gaelic influence had been at work in allotting these names. This, however, can scarcely have been the case, and the exceptional arrangement probably arises from one of two causes,—either the use of Quoy as a qualitative in English names, as Quoysmiddie, the smithy or forge by the quoy; or some obscure phonetic law, such as that which, in Gaelic, always places *sean*, old, before the word it qualifies. Quiràng, in Skye, written Cuidhrang in Gaelic, is *kvi rand*, round pen or paddock.

<small>Norse test words.</small> The surest test-syllables for Norse or Danish names are certain generic terms used as suffixes.

Fjall becomes in English "fell," as Goat Fell in Arran. Crìffel in Kirkcudbright is probably *kráka fjall*, crow-hill; the first vowel has been shortened by umlaut, but it is written Crafel in Pont's map. *Fjall* becomes *bhal* in Gaelic writing; so Còpeval in Harris is *kupu fjall*, cup-shaped hill.

Gnipa, a peak, remains as the Knipe, a hill near New Cumnock in Ayrshire; and perhaps as the Nappers, near Newton-Stewart in Galloway.

Klettr, a cliff. The final *r* is the sign of the masculine nominative singular, and disappears in composition. Brèaklet, near Campbeltown, is *breiða klettr*, broad cliff. Clàttranshaws, on the Kirkcudbright Dee, seems to be the same word, with M.E. *shaws*, woods, added.

Gil, a ravine, so common in our topography, is equivalent to the Scottish "cleuch"; and *dalr*, a dale, may easily be distinguished from the Gaelic *dal*, because while the latter invariably begins the name, as Dalrỳmple, the former always ends it, as Swòr-

Their Languages. 89

dale, in Lewis—*svarðar dalr*, the valley of the green sward.

Nes, a headland, often becomes *nish* in Gaelic, as Tròtternish in Skye and Trùddernish in Islay—*trylldir nes*, enchanted cape. Càithness, *Cata nes*, and Sìnniness in the Bay of Luce, are examples of this word from opposite ends of Scotland. Stènnis means *stein nes*, cape of the standing stones; but Gartnèss in Islay is Gaelic, *gart nan eas*, paddock at the waterfalls, and Aùchness in Wigtownshire, spelt Achinness in 1468, is also Gaelic—*each inis*, horse-pasture. Invernèss is, of course, the *inbher*, or mouth, of Adamnan's Nesa.

Hóp means primarily a sheltered bay, but by analogy it is used inland to signify any sheltered place, as Stànhope, the name of farms near Annan and Biggar—*stein hóp*, the stone shelter or glen; Kìrkhope in Selkirkshire and Dumfriesshire, the church glen; and Hòbkirk, formerly Hopekirk, near Hawick, the church in the hope or shelter.

Völlr, a field, generally becomes "wall" in composition, as Dìngwall in Ross-shire, and Tìngwall in Shetland—*þinga völlr*, the field of assembly; but it takes a slightly different form in Dumfriesshire and the Isle of Man—Tìnwald. Mòuswald in Dumfries-shire is *mosi völlr*, moss-field.

Vík is a word peculiarly Scandinavian, meaning a creek or small bay. The northern pirates took their name of Vikingr, or Vikings as we call them, from their habit of frequenting such inlets in the coast.

It can generally be distinguished in place-names from the common A.S. *wic*, a dwelling-place or town, from the position of the place. Prèstwick, indeed, near Ayr, might be either a bay or a dwelling; but we know it to be the latter, and that it signified *preost wic*, the priest's dwelling; for in Norse it would have been Papa-víc, to signify "priest's bay." Àscog in Bute, Àscock in Lorn, Portàskaig in Islay, have this word *vík* pretty well disguised: these names are from *askr vík*, ship's creek. The town of Wick was written Vik in 1140; but Hàwick has nothing to do with the sea, and means in old Northern English *haugh wick*, the town on the low pasture-land.

Bekkr, a rivulet, is not very common in Scotland, but it comes out as Ellerbeck and Waterbeck in Dumfriesshire; and Grèenbeck in the same county is probably *grünnr bekkr*, shallow brook.

It has already been explained how *fjörðr*, a firth, appears in different forms in such names as Bròadford, Sèaforth, Snìzort, and Mòydart; an equally puzzling name to follow is *vágr*, a creek, for it comes out as "voe" and then "way." Stòrnoway is *Stjarna vágr*, Stjarna's bay, and appears again as Loch Stòrnua in Kintyre. Mèavig, in Lewis and Harris, is *mjo-vágr*, narrow bay.

Vatn, a lake, becomes "vat," as Làngavat, the name of many a sheet of water in the Outer Hebrides, long lake.

Ey, an island, is generally easy to be recognised.

Their Languages. 91

The name Pàbay or Pàpa is attached to four islands in the Hebrides, one in Skye, two in Orkney, and three in Shetland: it is *pap ey*, priest's island, indicating early religious settlement. But St Kilda must be a corruption of the Gaelic: there never was a saint of that name, which probably represents *oilean celi Dé*, isle of the servants of God, or holy Culdees. But though the Norsemen have left no trace on St Kilda, there seems to be a distinct record of the pre-Celtic race in the name Dunfirbolg, the fort of the Firbolg or Iverians. Stàffa is Norse *stafa ey*, staff-island, from the columnar formation of the rocks; and Ulva, *ulfa ey*—wolf-island; Bèrnera, *Björnar ey*—Björni island, and so on.

Bœr or *by*, a village, farm, or dwelling, the origin of our Scots *byre*, is one of the Scandinavian terms least likely to be overlooked. It is not common in the northern isles, where the equivalent *bolstaðr* takes its place; hence *by* is supposed to mark occupation by the Dubh Gall or Danes, rather than by the Fingall or Norwegians. Sòroby in Tiree, Sòroba near Oban, Sòrby in Wigtownshire, Sòurby in Dumfriesshire and Cumberland; Bùsby near Glasgow, and in Perthshire, Wigtownshire, and three times in Ayrshire, are instances of this suffix. Kirkby or Kìrby—*kirkju by*, which occurs so commonly in England, is replaced in the Scottish Lowlands by A.S. Kìrkton, which is given upwards of fifty times in the Post Office Directory. Near Còrsbie in Wigtownshire is a farm called Barlàuchlane — *barr Lochlinn*, the

Norseman's hill; for the Vikings were also known as Lochlinn in Gaelic. Kirklàuchlane, in the same county, used to be written Kerclauchlinc, *cathair* (caher) or *ceathramhadh* (carrow) *Lochlinn*, the Norseman's fort or land quarter.

Bólstaðr, a farmhouse or dwelling, is equivalent to the Gaelic *baile*, the Welsh *trev*, the Saxon *tún* or *ham*. I have not identified this suffix in the southern counties, except in Wòlfstar in East Lothian, nor does it occur in the Isle of Man; hence it may be supposed to be Norse rather than Danish, for it is exceedingly common in the northern isles, where it takes most perplexing forms. In Shetland it appears singly as Bùsta, in Lewis as Bòsta, in Coll as Boust, and in Islay as Bòllsa. Càlbost in Lewis is *kald bólstaðr*, cold croft, like the Gaelic Balfòur—*baile fuar;* Gàrrabost, Geir's farm; Nìsabost in Harris and Skye, and Nèsbustar in Orkney, are *nes bólstaðr*, cape farm. Further south this word is more disguised in Cròssapool in Tiree—*krosa bólstaðr*, croft of the cross, Kìrkapoll in Mull, kirk farm, &c.; and in Islay it degenerates into *-bus*, as Còrnabus, corn-farm; Eòrabus, beach farm, equivalent to Killantràe, in Wigtownshire, from the Gaelic *ceathramhadh* (carrow) *an traigh*, land-quarter of the beach; Kìnnabus, *kinnar bólstaðr*, "cheek" farm, at the cheek or side of the hill.

Setr, a shieling or mountain pasture, equivalent to Gaelic *airidh*, I have not found in the south of Scotland, though it enters into names in the Isle of Man.

In Lewis it gives Lìnshader, flax croft, and Shèshader —*sœ setr*, shieling by the sea. In that island *setr* is written in Gaelic *seadair* (shadder); but in Orkney, where there is no Gaelic, it is always written *setter*.

Þ*weit*, a parcel of land cleared of wood, a paddock, which Canon Isaac Taylor enumerates forty-three times in Cumberland, is hardly to be found in Scotland, though it is very common both in Norway and Denmark as a suffix in place-names. Mùrraythwaite and Cràwthwaite in Dumfriesshire are the only Scottish examples I have noticed, though Professor Veitch says that Mòorfoot was written Murethwate in the old Border laws. It corresponds to the Welsh *llanerch*.

Þ*orpe*, a hamlet, is common at this day in Danish place-names, but is rare in Norway; hence it might be inferred that the Danes mustered strong and long in East Anglia and Westmoreland, where there are many thorpes. It is not found in Scotland; but we must be slow in deduction, for both "thwaite" and "thorpe" would soon pass out of use in Gaelic-speaking districts, because the Gael used not to pronounce *th*.

There is one test-word which may be looked for in vain in the topography of southern Scotland—namely, *fors*, modern *foss*, a waterfall. Even in the north, "land of the mountain and the flood," it is found but sparingly—as Forss near Thurso, Forse near Wick, perhaps Fòrres in Moray, and Foss near Pitlochry exhaust the list, so far as known to me.

This is the more strange, because in northern England "force" is the common name for a waterfall.

Time will not permit me to enter upon a minute examination of Norse prefixes; but there is one which I must mention, because it corresponds in form to two very different words, one in Anglo-Saxon, the other in modern English.

Bygg is the Norse for barley. Bìgholm, near Beith, was named with no reference to its size; had it been so, it would have been Meikleholm, just as we find Meikledale near Langholm, O.N. *mikill dalr*—for "big," signifying large, has no place in Scandinavian speech. Bìgholm, therefore, can only be the Norse *bygg holmr*, barley-land; for *holmr*, meaning primarily an island, means also low fertile land near water, just as do the A.S. *holm* and the Gaelic *inis*. The latter word becomes Inks (the name of meadows beside the river Cree), and Inch; and even the English "isle" is so applied sometimes, as Mìllisle, near Garlieston, where there is no island, only meadows. Bìggar, in Lanarkshire, was written Begart as late as 1524, and this name, as well as Bìggart near Beith and Bìggarts near Moffat, signifies *bygg garðr*, barley-field. The Anglo-Saxon for barley is *bere*, whence Beàrholm, a village in Lanarkshire, and probably Beàryards near Glasgow. It is not possible to decide whether Làngholm be A.S. or Norse, as the words are identical in both languages to denote the "long holm" or long pasture beside the river Esk.

Their Languages. 95

The other word for which the Norse *bygg*, barley, is very apt to be mistaken is the A.S. *byggan*, to build, still in use in Lowland Scots. The corresponding Norse word, *byggja*, though used in the same sense in the modern language, did not acquire it till the fourteenth or fifteenth century, previously to which it meant to settle or to live. Therefore the name Biggins may be safely assumed to be Anglo-Saxon or Lowland Scots, and so may the forty and odd Newbiggings which are given in the Post Office Directory. In the old Norse of the Sagas they always spoke of *reisa hús* or *göra hús*, never of *byggja hús*.

In this word *göra*, to make or build, there is some reason to trace the origin of a very old name which has puzzled many people. There is a district in Glasgow, as in many other towns, called the Gòrbals. Now in Orkney, so Jamieson affirms, *gorback* is a local word for a kind of rampart, which seems to be the same word, both being a contraction of *görr balkr*, built walls, a breastwork. It is to be regretted that the authorities of Newton-Stewart, when lately they put up names to their streets, seem to have thought this a vulgar name, for they have re-christened the Gorbals Queen Street.

There is perhaps no district in Scotland where the intermixture of languages is so perplexing as in the southern part of Strathclyde, round the watershed where the Clyde, Tweed, and Annan take their source. Names appear here on the map like fossils,

Intermixture of languages in Strathclyde.

with this important difference, however, that whereas geological remains are found lying in successive strata, showing their relative antiquity, here we have Celtic, Saxon, and Scandinavian names deposited on a uniform plane, and we are obliged to rely on the uncertain light of early history whereby to estimate their age.

It is tantalising to examine Ptolemy's list of names in southern Scotland, and realise how very few of the scanty list can be identified with existing names. Of these *Novios flumen* may certainly be taken as the Nith, beyond which to the west dwelt the Picts known as Niduarian. Nith, then, is the survival of a name conferred on the river before A.D. 120, but we know not in what language it is. Perhaps it is one of those pre-Celtic Iverian names which baffle our curiosity. Some of Ptolemy's river names are clearly Celtic. Thus Abravannus, a name he gives to a river corresponding in position to the Luce, in Wigtownshire, is obviously no more than *aber amhuinn* (avon), river mouth, with a Greek suffix.

We may assume that the oldest speech we have to deal with in southern Strathclyde is Gaelic or Pictish, that next in antiquity is the Welsh dialect, after which came Anglo-Saxon, and, last of all foreign tongues, the Norse. But it would not be safe to assume that Benyèllary—*beinn iolaire*, the eagle's hill, and Petillery, both in Galloway, are older names than Earn Craig in Strathclyde, with the same

Their Languages. 97

meaning, for Gaelic was spoken in Galloway centuries after Anglo-Saxon was the settled speech of Dumfriesshire and Lanark. Nor again would it be a certain inference that, because Anglo-Saxon settlements preceded those of the Norsemen on the Scottish Border, therefore it follows that the Anglo-Saxon Earn Craig is older than the Norse Yearn Gill, *örn gil*, which is the name of a hill in the same range; for this reason, that A.S. *œrn*, an eagle, became, and still remains, part of the vernacular, just as did the Norse *gil*, a ravine; so the name Earn Craig may have been bestowed at any time during the last 1300 years. It is, in fact, exactly the name that would be given by a Clydesdale or Ettrick shepherd of to-day to denote an eagle's crag.

A whole chapter might be written on the use of the Celtic prefix *dal* and the Teutonic suffix *dale*. The former is peculiar to Scottish topography, and is quite distinct in meaning from, though of cognate origin with, the latter. *[Difference between Norse dalr and Gaelic dal.]*

The Gaelic *dal* means a portion of land, the separate possession of a tribe, family, or individual.

The Saxon *dæl* means a portion or share, but not of land more than anything else, and was not used in the early topography of that people.

The Norse *dalr* is a dale or valley, a piece of land separated from the rest of the country, not by human arrangement, but by hills forming the valley. From a common root come a number of words, all containing the same idea of "cleft" or separation. In

English we have received through Anglo-Saxon "deal" (to share out), "dole" (what is dealt), "deal" (as in the phrase "a great deal"), "deal" (a thin board of timber from the division of a tree). Through the Norse we have received "dale" and "dell."

In Ireland of old the word *dal* bore the special meaning of a "tribe"—either a community separated from the rest of the people, or occupying land set apart for their use. But it is not now to be found on Irish maps; it has completely disappeared with the tribal system, which is all the more remarkable seeing that nine *dals* are mentioned in the 'Annals of the Four Masters,' one of which was transplanted to Scotland in the fifth century by Fergus Mór, the son of Erc, when he led his followers to settle in Alban or Caledonia. By the natives this colony was called after the invaders *Airer Gaedhil*, in modern Gaelic *Earra Gaidheal*, the boundary or territory of the Gael, which is now shortly pronounced Argỳle; but the colonists themselves named it Dalriàda, after their native Dalriada in Antrim—that is, *dal righe fhada*, land of (Cairbre with) the long arm, or, as some prefer, *dal righ fhada*, land of the tall king (Cairbre).

In that part of Scotland which lies nearest to Ireland, *dal* is of common occurrence: twenty-seven names having this prefix have been catalogued in Galloway alone, and nearly every other Scottish county affords instances of it.

The historic family of Dalrymple take their name from a piece of land in Ayrshire. A visit to this place shows how accurately the locality was described —*dal chruim puill*, land of the curved pool, for there the river Doon wellnigh encircles a level piece of fertile land. Dalry, in Ayrshire, Mid-Lothian, Kirkcudbright, Argyleshire, and Perthshire, is probably rightly interpreted *dal righ*, king's land: in the county last mentioned this name is alternatively written Dalrigh and Dalree, for, being in a Highland district, the correct pronunciation of the last syllable has been preserved, instead of adopting the modern value of *y* (eye). Dalnacàrdoch in Inverness-shire is *dal na ceardaich*, land of the forge, equivalent to Smithycroft near Millerston in the suburbs of Glasgow; Dalintòbar in Argyleshire—*dal an tiobair*, land of the well, just as we have Wellcroft near Sorby in Wigtownshire; Dalnaspìdal in Perthshire—*dal na spidail*, land of the hospital, like Spital Farm near Lochgelly in Fife.

That is the invariable meaning of *dal* as a prefix in Gaelic names, though, to be sure, it must not be forgotten that Dalmèny was spelt Dunmanyn in 1250, and was probably a fort of the Picts of Manann, who have left their name in Slamànnan.

Now, let us see the difference of *dale* as a suffix. In the northern islands of course it is the Norse *dalr*, a valley—directly named by the Norsemen. Làxdale in Lewis and Làcasdle in Harris are the same as Laxadalr in Iceland, salmon-river dale.

Làxdale also occurs in Orkney, where there are no salmon, but plenty of big sea-trout, which the Norsemen called by the same name.

So in Cumberland and Westmoreland, Bòrrodail —*borgh dalr*, castle dale, and Kèndal—dale of the Kent; such names being probably pure Norse, without Anglo-Saxon intervention. And again in Galloway the names as Kilquhòckadale and Glenstòckadale show that the Norsemen gave names to these farms, and then the Gael came back and prefixed *gleann* and *coill*, the glen and the wood.

Norse and Saxon loanwords.

But many of our Lowland names ending in *dale* originated after the Norse *dalr* had passed into the Saxon speech, and it was applied to places long after the Norsemen had been sent to the rightabout. Nithsdale, for instance, is written Stranid in 1350—*srath Nid*. Annandale has the Welsh form Estrahannent in the twelfth century, and also the Gaelic Stratanant, and it is not till 1295 that it appears as Anandresdale. So although *dale* is a Norse word, it is not safe to predicate of all names ending in dale that they are of Norse origin.

But it is otherwise when one language has passed away without lending words to its successor. Thus in the Lowlands stream-names like—

Dòuglas = *dubh glas*,
Dìpple = *dubh pol*,
Doon = *dubh amhuinn*,
Dusk = *dubh uisc*,
} black water,

must be of higher antiquity than the synonymous

Black Burns and Blackwaters which are in almost every parish.

So Prièstgill on Douglas Water must be of later date than Glentàggart on the opposite side of the stream; and though Prìesthope on the Tweed and Prìestgill on the Clyde have Norse suffixes, we know that these names are no more than medieval, for if they had been pure Norse the name would have been Papahope and Papgill.

Some names in Strathclyde may be accurately dated. In 1156 Henry II. of England expelled a number of Flemings who had settled in his realm. They found refuge in Scotland, and it is to Thancard and Lambin that Thànkerton and Làmington owe their names. Sỳmington, in Ayrshire and Lanarkshire, both took their name from Simon Lockhart or Loccard about the same time.

Among Saxon and Norse words which form part of the living dialect, of which, when they occur in place-names, the age cannot be even approximately fixed, are the following:—

Norse.

Grain, the branch of a river, *grein*, a branch, as Tròwgrain, the trough branch, in Roxburghshire. Countrymen still speak of the "grains" of a fork.

Fell, a hill, *fjall*, as Fell of Barhùllion in Wigtownshire, where this word is prefixed to the older Gaelic— *barr chuilean*, hill of the whelps.

Hope, a shelter, *hóp*, as Tòdhope, in Dumfriesshire, the fox's shelter.

Shiel, a hut, *skáli*, as in Sèlkirk, the shiel kirk.
Haugh, a low-lying pasture, *hagi*, as the Haughs of Urr.

Anglo-Saxon.

Syke, a runnel.
Law, a hill, as Grèenlaw.
Dod, a hill.
Coomb, a valley, common on Eskdalemuir.
Swire, a neck, as Manor Swire on Tweed; The Swire, near Dumfries; Swarehead, Kirkcudbright.
Lane, a sluggish stream, as Lanebrèddan, in the Stewartry of Kirkcudbright, a name which shows that the Gaelic-speaking population had adopted the word *lane*, for Lanebrèddan means A.S. or N. *lane*, Gaelic *bradan*, a salmon — *i.e.*, the salmon-burn, a place where salmon still run up to spawn in from the Dee.

LECTURE V.

THE LESSON OF PLACE-NAMES.

SUCCESSION OF RACES NOT EXPLAINED BY PLACE-NAMES—THESE ILLUSTRATE FORMER APPEARANCE OF THE COUNTRY—THE OLD FOREST—ITS TREES AND UNDERGROWTH—HUMBLER VEGETATION—CROPS—ANIMALS LOCALLY OR GENERALLY EXTINCT—THE CHASE—DEER AND OTHER ANIMALS—NAMES OF ANIMALS BORNE BY MEN.

THE conclusions to which, by a study of place-names, we are brought as to the ancient ethnography of Scotland, and the successive prevalence of one or other of its inhabitant races, are, it must be admitted, somewhat precarious. After all, although it is easy to recognise the various layers of language deposited by successive occupation, the most that they afford is evidence confirming the narrative of history. I, at least, must confess myself unable to extract from the place-names of Scotland any further knowledge of early history than has been prepared for us by the

Succession of races not explained by place-names.

monumental works of the late Mr Skene. So cautious was he in speculation, so diligent in comparison of authorities, so luminous in his conclusions, that he has made it a very difficult task for any one to add to the store of historical knowledge which he amassed and imparted to the public. In carrying out research into the meaning of place-names, when one comes upon the footprint of Mr Skene, so far from being discouraged, one feels confident of being on the right track.

Information as to the land and its inhabitants.

But if the light reflected from place-names upon the page of history is uncertain, it is otherwise with that thrown by them upon the appearance of the country in ancient times and the occupation of its inhabitants. The forest has been swept from our hillsides and plains, and were it not for the record contained in place-names, memory of the greenwood would be preserved only by the blackened trunks and roots in the peat-mosses. When Dr Johnson visited Scotland, he vowed that during the whole of his northern tour he saw but three trees big enough to hang a man on; and although since that day large breadths of land have been planted up, the general character of our scenery is the reverse of sylvan. It is interesting, therefore, to trace, even in the districts now most treeless, the record not only of the departed woodland, but of the very species of trees which composed it.

Woods and trees.

The commonest word for a wood in old Gaelic is *coill* (Manx *keeyll*), but in modern Gaelic this is *coille* (killy). It is fair, therefore, to assume that of two forms of the same compound, Culmòre and Killiemòre, two places in Wigtownshire, the first is older by some centuries, representing *coill mór*, great wood; the second being medieval, *coille mór*. *Coill* usually gives the prefix Cul- or Kil- in Anglicised names, but is not always to be distinguished from *cill*, a church, *cuil*, a corner, *cul*, a hill-back, and *caol*, a strait or narrow place. The following instances from a single county, Wigtownshire, illustrate the confusion arising between these words in rendering Gaelic pronunciation into English letters:—

Culmòre . . .	*coill mór*, great wood.
Killiemòre . .	*coille mór*, great wood.
Kilmòrie . . .	*cill Muire*, Mary's church (locative case of *ceall*).
Killantràe, 1582 Kerantra, Kerintraye	*ceathramhadh an traigh*, land-quarter of the shore.
Kildròchat, *earlier* Kerodròched *and* Kernadrochat	*ceathramhadh an drochid*, land-quarter of the bridge.

The last name, Kildròchat, is peculiarly instructive, because it might so easily be assumed that it was the same as Kindròchit in Aberdeen and Perthshire—*cinn drochid*, at the bridge head, *tête-du-pont* —and Kindròught in Banff, and it is only the old spellings which reveal the true etymology.

As a suffix, *coill* generally takes the aspirate, as in Barwhill, *barr chuill*, and Auchenhill, *achadh na chuill*, both in Galloway, the hill-top and field of the wood. But it must be admitted that in this position *coill* cannot be distinguished from *coll*, genitive *chuill*, a hazel, so Barwhìll and Auchenhìll might mean the hill-top and field of the hazel-bush. The modern Gaelic for hazel is *calltunn*, which accounts for many places in Galloway called Càldons. Càlton occurs in Ayrshire, Stirlingshire, and Argyleshire, as well as attached to a well-known hill in Edinburgh and a district in Glasgow; but it is necessary to examine old spellings to determine where this represents the Gaelic *calltun*, hazels, or the Anglian *cauld tún*.

Hazel-nuts were an important article of food in primitive times. When a small loch at Dirvàird (*dobhur* or *doire bhaird* (vaird), the bard's water or wood), near Glenluce, was drained some ten years ago, there was found a large crannog or lacustrine dwelling, which, by reason of the collapse of the woodwork, had sunk below the water-level. The north-east shore of the lake, which, according to the prevailing south-west wind, was the usual lee-shore, was covered with many cart-loads of broken hazel-nut shells, which had drifted thither from the island, the remains of the repast of these lake-dwellers·

Coillte, the plural of *coill*, a wood, comes out as the name Cults in Aberdeenshire, Fife, and Wigtownshire, as Kèlty in Perthshire and Kinross, as Cult in Perth and Linlithgow, and Quils in Perthshire. Cultmìck in Wigtownshire is *coillte muic*, the swine-woods; but Cultùllich in Perthshire must be read *cul tulaich*, back of the hill.

Their Lesson.

The derivative *coillín*, woodland, produces Cùllen in Banff and Lanarkshire; and another form, *coilleachan*, gives Quìllichan on the Findhorn.

The usual Anglo-Saxon for wood was *wudu* (becoming *wode* in Middle English), which probably gives the suffix in names like Aìket near Annan and Aìtket in North Ayrshire—*ác wudu*, Bìrket near Dalry—*beorc wudu*, birch wood, and Blàiket near Dumfries—*blœc wudu*, black wood. A small wood was *scaga*, whence our "shaw," as Bìrkshaw near Dumfries and Bìrkenshaw in Lanarkshire.

The usual Gaelic name for a tree is *craebh* (craev or crew), which appears most often as a suffix, as Auchencròw in Berwickshire, Auchencrùive near Ayr—*achadh na craebh*, field of trees. Sometimes the prefix drops off, as Crùivie, a ruinous castle in the parish of Logie, Fife, which was once *caiseal craebhe* (creuvie), castle of the tree, which appellation remains entire in Castle Crèavie, a place in Kirkcudbrightshire. Knockcràvie and Corncràvie, in the same county, are *cnoc* and *corán craobhach* or *craobhe*, wooded hill or hill of the tree.

There cannot, of course, be any trace in ancient topography of the hundreds of exotic species with which the diligence of collectors has enabled us to adorn our scenery. We shall look in vain for allusion in place-names to the chestnut, beech, walnut, plane, sycamore, larch, lime, or laurel, for none of these are indigenous to North Britain; indeed the list of native trees is a very limited one.

The oak.   The oak was in early times, as it is now, the most important timber-tree. It entered largely into the construction of artificial islands, called crannogs, from *crann*, a tree, and may still be dug thence and from our mosses, hard and serviceable after centuries of submersion, while other native species, though preserving their shape, have become as soft as cheese. Canoes are often found from 20 to 40 feet in length, invariably hollowed out of solid oak-trunks.

The old Irish word for oak was *daur*, in the genitive *dara* or *darach*, which has been taken as the modern Gaelic name, while in Manx and Welsh it remains *dar*. In Aberdeenshire and Dumfriesshire the old word remains in the name Deer, while Dàrra and Dàrroch, in Aberdeenshire, Stirlingshire, and elsewhere, show the modern form.

There is a notable instance in the 'Book of Deer' of an attempt to explain a place-name artistically. When Columba parted with Drostan, the latter, it is recorded, shed tears, whereupon Columba exclaimed, "Let Dear be the name of the place hereafter," a pun on the Gaelic *deur*, a tear. Aikiehill and Aikeybrae, in the parish of Deer, are much more faithful tokens of the true meaning of the name. Kildàrroch in Ayrshire and Wigtownshire is *coill darach*, oak-wood, equivalent to A.S. Aiket; but Culdèrry in Wigtownshire must be regarded as *cúl doire*, back of the wood.

The word *doire* gives the name to many places all over Scotland, from Sutherland to Galloway, usually with the definite article prefixed—the Dèrry or the

Dèrries. It is a derivative of *daur*, meaning strictly an oak-wood, but more generally any wood or thicket. Dirriemòre, a high mountain-pass in Ross-shire, is *doire mór*, great wood, though the trees have long since passed away. Lòndonderry in Ireland is written Daire-Calgaich in the 'Annals,' and Adamnan, writing in the seventh century, translated the name *roboretum Calgachi*, Calgach's oak-wood. It received the prefix of "London" to distinguish it from other places called Derry, on account of the property acquired there by London merchants.

Time will not permit me to dwell upon thousands of place-names formed from other trees: I may mention, however, that *beith* (bey), the birch, which is easily recognised with its unaspirated initial in Drumbàe, the birch-ridge, becomes "vey" under aspiration, as in Auchenvèy and Largvèy in Galloway—*achadh na bheith*, birch-field, and *leary bheith*, birch-hillside. Beith and Barbèth in Ayrshire preserve the final aspirated dental, which came easily to the Welsh-speaking people of Strathclyde, but was a sound which the Gael was incapable of uttering. Beòch in Ayrshire, Galloway, and Dumfriesshire is *beitheach* (beyagh), birch-land, equivalent to A.S. Bìrket, *beorc wudu*. *Uinnse* (inshy), the ash, becomes Inshaw Hill in Wigtownshire, and the plural, *uinnsean* (inshan), takes the peculiar form of Inshanks, the name of two places in that county, and Inshewan, near Kirriemuir; while the common alternative form, *uinnseog* (inshog), remains as Inshock in Forfarshire, Inshaig

The birch.

The ash.

in Argyleshire, Inshog near Nairn; and Drumnamìnshog and Knocknìnshock in Kirkcudbrightshire are respectively the ridge and the hill of the ash-trees. Killymìnshaw in Dumfriesshire is no doubt *coille nam uinnse,* or ash-wood.

The aspen. The aspen, or "quakin' ash" of Lowland Scots, is *criothach* (creeagh) in Gaelic, and gives the name to Creich in Sutherland, Ross, Argyle, and Wigtown, and perhaps to Crieff in Perthshire; and the plural, *criothachean,* appears as Crèechan in Dumfriesshire and Wigtownshire. Crianlàrich, a well-known station on the Callander and Oban line, may be either *crich* or *criothach na laraich,* the boundary or the aspen-tree at the house-site.

The elm. I must ask you to enter more closely into examination of the elm — not the well-known species known as the English elm (*Ulmus campestris*), which is not indigenous, having been introduced by the Romans, but the wych-elm (*Ulmus montana*), a tree which has given the name to many well-known places. The old Gaelic name for it was *leam* (lam), plural, *leaman.* Ptolemy's *Leamanonius Lacus* is now Loch Lòmond, the lake of the elms, out of which flows the Lèven, which is the aspirated form *leamhan* (lavan); and it is interesting to find these two forms again side by side in Fife, where are the Lomond Hills overlooking the town of Leven.[1] The Lennox,

---

[1] The two forms come together again in Warwickshire, where not far from Leamington is Levenhull—*leamhan choill,* elm-wood, and, in the same neighbourhood, a place called Elmdon.

a district formerly written Levenax, is the adjectival form *leamhnach* (lavnah), an elm-wood; and in England the river Leam, giving its name to Leamington, the Leven in Cumberland, the Lune in Lancashire (Alauna of Ptolemy), and in Ireland the Laune at Killarney, must all have once been named *amhuinn leamhan*, elm-river. *Leamh chuill* (lav whill), elm-wood, appears as Barlùel in Galloway, the hill-top of the elm-wood; the derivative *leamhraidhean* (lavran or lowran), elm-wood, becomes Lòwran and Lòwring, also in Galloway; and in the same province I have picked up an alternative form to *leamhan*, common in Ireland — namely, *sleamh* (slav) and *sleamhan* (slavvan), whence the names Craigslàve and Craigsloùan. Yet another derivative, *leamhreach* (lavrah), seems to be the origin of Caerlàverock, *cathair* (caher) *leamhreaich*, fortress in the elm-wood.

Another fertile source of Scottish place-names is the alder, Gaelic *fearn*, Welsh *gwern*, of which mention has already been made as the origin of Nairn, *amhuinn na' fhearn* (ern). The plural, *fearnan*, gives Fèrnan in Perthshire and Aberdeenshire; *fearnach*, abounding in alders, yields Fàrnoch and Feàrnoch in Argyleshire, Fèrnie in Fife, and Fèrnaig in Rossshire; while *fearnachan*, an alder-wood,[1] survives in Drumfàrnachan in Galloway, where also is found the aspirated form, Drumèarnachan.

The Anglo-Saxon *alr* and the Norse *ölr* produce the

The alder.

---

[1] *Fearnachan* in modern Gaelic means sloes, and this may be the reference in these names.

names of Allarstocks and Allarton, near Glasgow; Allarshaw, in Lanarkshire; Ellerslie, near Dumfries; Ellerbeck, near Ecclefechan; and Elderslie, in Renfrew.

The elder. The elder was *trom* of old, whence the Truim, a tributary of the Spey, formerly *amhuinn truim*, river of the elder-bush; but the modern word is *troman*, Manx *tramman*, which gives the name to Tràmmond Ford, on the estuary of the Cree in Galloway, at one end of which ford is Castràmont, which, despite its Roman complexion, is merely *cas tromain*, foot of the elder (ford). Several places are also named from the Anglo-Saxon and Old Northern English name of the elder—bourtree.

The willow. *Saileach*, a willow, gives names to many places, as Sàlachan in Argyleshire, *saileachean*, the willows; Sàlachry in the same county, *saileachreach*, a place of willows, which appears as Sàuchrie in Ayrshire; Barsàlloch and Barnsàllie in Wigtownshire, *barr na saileach*, willow-hill. But Barnshàlloch in Kirkcudbright is *barr an sealghe* (shallughy), hill of the hunting. Drimnasàllie, near Fort William, is ridge of the willows.

A.S. *sealh* produces M.E. *salwe*, our "sallow," whence the Scots word "sauch" and the place-name Sàuchie.

The rowan. *Caorunn* (keerun), the mountain-ash or rowan-tree, is generally aspirated in compound names, as Attachoirrin in Islay, the rowan-tree house; Leachd a' chaoruinn on the shore of Loch Ossian in Corrour

Their Lesson. 113

Forest, and Barwhìrran in Wigtownshire, rowan-tree hill.

Gìus or *giuthas* (gyuse), the Scots fir, is pretty well disguised in Loch Goosie in Kirkcudbright—*loch giuthasach*, lake of the firs; but is easily recognised in Gùisachan in Inverness-shire, and Kingùssie—*cinn giuthasaich*, at the head of the firwood. <small>The fir.</small>

From *iubhar* (yure), the yew, comes Urie in Aberdeenshire; *iubharach*, a yew-wood, Palnùre in Kirkcudbright; *pol na' iubhar*, yew-stream, Glenùre in Argyleshire and Coire-iubhair in Inverness-shire. <small>The yew.</small>

Innumerable names take their rise from black and white thorns.

Skeòch in Stirlingshire, Ayrshire, and Dumfriesshire, Skeòg, Scaith, and Skate in Wigtownshire, represent *sceach*, *sgitheach*, or *sgitheog*, as the hawthorn is variously written in Gaelic; and the Anglo-Saxon Thornhill in Dumfriesshire and Stirlingshire has its exact counterpart in Drumskeòg and Barskeòch in Galloway. <small>The hawthorn.</small>

The blackthorn is *draieghean* (dreean), Manx *drine*, Welsh *draen*, but the older form in Cormac's Glossary is *droigen*, which we find unimpaired in Mildrìggan, an estate in Wigtownshire. This is a hybrid of Saxon and Gaelic, for in a charter of 1674 it stands as Drèggan Mylne—the Mill of Dreggan, *i.e., droigen*. It is still a great place for blackthorns: the archaic form of the name shows it to be one of the oldest in the country, and testifies to <small>The blackthorn.</small>

H

the length of time that this bush has clung to the spot. Dranniemànner in Kirkcudbrightshire is *draighean na mainir*, the blackthorns of the goat-pen, which has its parallel in the next county, Wigtownshire, as Drangòwer (written by Pont Drongangower) — *draigheanan gobhar* (drannan gowr), blackthorns of the goats.

Other names of the same origin are—

Dràinie, a parish in Elgin.
Dr̀ynie, in Ross-shire.
Drònach, on the Perthshire Almond.
Dr̀ynachan, on the Findhorn.
Dr̀ynoch, in Skye.
Dron, a parish in Perthshire.
Dròngan and Auchendràin, } in Ayrshire.
Dundrènnan, Drùngan, Drònnan, and Drannandòw, } in Kirkcudbright.

Bardràin, near Paisley, has its exact translation in Slàethorn-rig in Barr, Ayrshire.

The bramble.

Dreas (drass), a bramble, genitive *dris*, produces the adjective *drisach*, whence Drìsaig, Ardrìshaig, Drumdrìsaig, and Bardrìshach, all in Argyleshire, and Glendrìssock in Ayrshire; while from the fruit of the bramble, *smeur* (smerr), come Sron-smeur, blackberry-hill, in Rannoch Forest, Smòorage in Lamlash Bay, Slewsmìrroch—*sliabh smeurach*, blackberry moor—in Wigtownshire, and Smirle in the same county, representing two adjectival forms, *smeurach* and *smeurlach*.

From *dealg* (dallig), a thorn, we get the plural *dealghe* (dalhy), whence Dailly in Ayrshire and Kirkcudbright, and Dally in Wigtownshire. Drumdàlly and Clamdàlly, both in Galloway, are *druim dealg* and *claon dealg*, thorny ridge and slope.

The great Highland district of Rànnoch takes its name from a lowly herb. The old Gaelic *raith* (ray), *raithan* (rahan), bracken fern, becomes *raithneach* in the modern language; thus Drumràe in Wigtownshire, *druim raith*, represents an older nomenclature than Drumràny in Ayrshire, *druim raithneach*, both signifying "fern-hill." The use of the character *z* to represent the old Scots consonantal *y*, which confuses English people in the pronunciation of such names as Càdzow (cadyo), Mènzies (mingis), and Dalziel (dee-ell), has prevailed to alter the pronunciation of Glen Rànza in Arran from the original *gleann raithneach*, ferny glen; and Blawràiny in Kirkcudbright has a meteorological complexion concealing the meaning of *blar raithneach*, ferny field. Rànna in Aberdeenshire, and Rànnas and Rànnochan in Moray, also derive their names from the bracken fern.

Aspiration greatly alters the forms assumed in composition by *fraoch* (freugh, frew), heather, and *feur*, grass. The Ford of Frew is on the Forth, about six miles above Stirling, well known of old as the place where the Highland caterans used to cross the sluggish channel; Freugh in Wigtownshire and

Argyleshire is another spelling, and Freùchie in Perthshire and Fife is *fraochach*, a heathery place. But in the genitive, *fhraeich* (hree), the *f* is usually aspirated, as Auchenrèe, near Blair Atholl,[1] and again near Portpatrick, which has nothing to do with *righ*, a king, but is perhaps *achadh an fhraeich*, heather field. Cretanrèe in Banff is *croit an fhraeich*, heather croft. Seeing that heather was the commonest natural growth on Scottish hill and dale before cultivation became general, it may seem strange why certain localities should be distinguished by allusion to that plant. The explanation is found in the high antiquity of such names, pointing to a time when the greater part of the land was under forest, and heather only grew in the open glades. *Feur*, grass, also loses the sound of the initial consonant in the genitive, and gives Strathỳre, *srath fheoir*, the grassy valley.

Clover.   *Saimir* or *seamrog* is the white clover, whence Glenchàmber in Wigtownshire, as the map-makers write it, mistaking the local pronunciation for the Scottish word "chalmer," a chamber. The alternative for *seamrog* gives Glenshìmerock in Kirkcudbright and Glenshàmrock in Ayrshire.

[1] This explanation is very doubtful. Auchenrèe in Blair Atholl is locally pronounced *rhŭee*, and is understood to mean *achadh an rhuidh* or *ruith*, field of the shieling. This name is, therefore, an example of the danger of interpreting Gaelic names imperfectly rendered phonetically in English characters, without listening to the local pronunciation. If this explanation be correct, then the suffix of Auchenrèe and Aìrdrie would represent the same word—one name meaning field of the shieling, the other the high shieling or pasture.

Aittin (atten), gorse or juniper, may be recognised Furze or juniper. in Dunèaton in the Upper Ward of Lanarkshire, —*dún aitten,* fort or hill of the whins or juniper; while a stream running near this place preserves the Welsh form *eithin,* the Nèthan, joining the Clyde at Cambusnèthan, being *afon eithin,* the river of the whins or juniper.

Giolc (gilk), in modern Gaelic *cuilc* (kuleg), pro- Broom. perly means a reed or cane; but the nomenclature of the humbler vegetation is somewhat slippery, and this word is commonly applied to the broom. Knockgìlsie and Knockgùlsha in Galloway are *cnoc giolcach,* the exact equivalent of Broomieknowe or Broomknowe, a name which is given twelve times in the Post Office Directory, or Broomhills, which appears there forty times. Auchengilshie, in Wigtownshire and Ayrshire, is the Gaelic for Broomfield, which appears eighteen times.

The usual name for a rush is *luachair,* which Rushes. survives unchanged in the Lòchar Moss, that great expanse of peat between Dumfries and Annan, and in Glenlòchar, the rushy glen, near Castle Douglas. It may also enter into names like Barlòckhart and Drumlòckhart in Galloway; but here it is possible that *lucart,* a big house, may have something to do with it. Pitlòchrie is probably *pett luacharach,* rushy croft.

Before leaving the vegetable kingdom we may Crops. glance at some traces of early cultivation. *Coirce* (kurkya), oats, has already been shown to be the

118   *Scottish Land-Names.*

origin of Barnkìrk and Barnkìrky in Galloway; in the same district the word is found in another form, Culquhìrk, the corner of oats, and Awhìrk, the oatfield. Similarly *eorna* (yorna), barley, comes out as Culhòrn, and may be compared with Coolnahòrna in Waterford and Wexford.

Another important crop in early times was flax, in Gaelic *lìn*. Port Leen, in Loch Ryan, marks a place where it was shipped, and Lochenalìng, in Wigtownshire, a place where it was steeped; Drumlèan, in Stirlingshire, and Glenlìng, in Wigtownshire, places where it was grown. Ochteralìnachan, near Stranraer, is *uachdarach lìnachan*, the upper flax-field. No flax is grown in these districts now.

Seagal (shaggul), rye, gives names like Auchenshùgle, near Glasgow, and Knockshòggle in Ayrshire; while root-crops, like carrots or turnips, were called *meacan* (maakan), yielding Blairmàkin, near Wigtown.

Extinct animals.   It would be impossible within reasonable limits of time to go over the list of animals which have left their names attached to places in our country; but there is some interest in examining names commemorating beasts and birds which are either wholly extinct or are confined to limited spaces within the realm.

The chase.   Hunting took precedence of farming as the occupation of the early inhabitants; hence *sealg* (shallug),

Their Lesson. 119

the chase, and terms connected with it, enter largely into Scottish place-names.

It has been surmised that the name Selgovæ, by which the Picts of Galloway were known, may be derived from *sealg*, and that they were thus distinguished as the "hunters." Barnshàlloch, Drumshàlloch, Glenshàlloch, and Kittyshàlloch, all in Galloway, and Cuttyshàllow in Ayrshire, are the *barr* or hill, the *druim* or ridge, the glen and the *ceide* (keddy) or hill-face of the hunting, just as Benshàlag in Nairn, Glenshèllach near Oban, Knockshèllie in Ayrshire; but Auchnashàlloch in Ross-shire and Argyleshire means the field of the willows. There are also farms called Shàlloch in Ayrshire and Banff; but this must not be confused with Chàlloch, a common name in Galloway, which is a corruption of *tealach*, a forge, just as in the same province *tiobar*, a well, becomes "chipper." Castle Shell in Wigtownshire is by local tradition affirmed to be an old hunting-seat; and the old name for the Moor of Edinburgh, where the king's hunt was held, was Drumsèlch. Hence the reddendo or rent for the barony of Penicuik was the blowing of six blasts *in cornu flatili*, on a hunting-horn. The old name Drumselch is now written Drumsheugh.

The hunting-horn itself was known as *adhairce* (aharky); one may almost hear the echoes of it still round Mulwhàrker, a hill in the Forest of Buchan, in Galloway—*maol adhairce*, hill of the hunting-horn—close to which is Hunt Ha', where the Earls of Cassilis used to lodge in pursuit of the red-deer. Slewnàrk, near Portpatrick, is probably *sliabh n'adhairce*, moor of the hunting-horn.

Deer.

The favourite beast of the chase was the red-deer, for which the usual word was *fiadh* (feeah); but it is not easily to be distinguished in composition from *fithach* (feeah), a raven. It is difficult to say at this day whether Craigenvèoch in Wigtownshire, Craigenfèoch near Paisley, and Craignafèoch near Greenock mean the deer's or, as is more probable, the raven's crag. Names ending in -*nee* generally represent the aspirated genitive *fhiaidh* (ee), of a deer, with the article, and these may be found in districts where the red-deer have long ceased to exist. Thus in Galloway we have Palnèe—*pol an fhiaidh*, the deer's stream—Craiginèe, and Drumanèe, the last occurring also as a place-name in Derry, Ireland.

From *eilid*, a hind, genitive *eilte*, come the names Kilhìlt, in Wigtownshire, written Kylnahilt in the Rotuli Scot., 1455—*coill na heilte*, wood of the hind; Craignèlder and Carnèltoch are in the mountains of Galloway—the craig and the cairn or hill of the hinds.

Names of animals borne by men.

Of course, in considering these names, it must be kept in mind that it was the practice among the Celts, as in most other semi-civilised communities, to distinguish men by the names of animals. Reginald of Durham narrates how one of the four monks who bore the body of St Cuthbert to the tomb had been detected in hiding a cheese from his brethren, and therefore he and his descendants were known by the name of Tod, *quod vulpeculam sonat*, "which means a fox-cub." Similarly in Ireland the family of Mac-Shinnagh—*mac sionaich*, son of the fox—took the name of Fox, in conformity with the law prohibiting the use of the Irish language within the Pale.

In the names last quoted, Kylnahilt and Craignelder, the presence of the article, shown by the *n* before the suffix, proves that it was an animal, and not an individual, after which these places were named.

The article does not occur in Strath Ossian in Perthshire, yet it most likely means in old Gaelic the strath of the red-deer calves or fawns, *srath oisin*—though that was a name sometimes borne by men. Scotsmen claim Ossian as a native bard, but he was really an Irish soldier-poet of the third century, named *oisin*, the fawn.

The alternative form *os* (osh), genitive *ois* (ish), gives Craignìsh in Ayrshire, which may be compared with Glenish in County Monaghan, written by the Annalists Glen ois; but Craignish in Argyleshire is written Cragginche in 1434 and Creginis in 1609, which looks like *creag innse*, rock in the meadow. The genitive plural, *os*, gives Glenòse in Skye and Glenhòise (pronounced Glenhòsh) in Kirkcudbright, the glen of the fawns; but this, again, is liable to confusion with *shuas* (hosh), upper, for Barhòise (pronounced Barhòsh) in Wigtownshire may be *barr shuas*, upper or north hill.

The modern Gaelic for roe is *earba*, but the old word was *earb*, and *earboc* was the roe-buck, preserved in Glenàrbuck near Bowling and Drumnàrbuck in Wigtownshire. The Norse *rá* and A.S. *ra*, especially the latter, enter into many names of places, in some of which the roe is never seen now. Ràeden, near Aberdeen, is A.S. *ra denn*, the roe's lair or sleeping-place; other examples are Ràehills in Dumfriesshire, Ràelees near Selkirk, &c., the latter being of similar origin to the English surname Raleigh or Rayleigh. But unless the stress is carefully noted, this prefix is sure to be confused with the Gaelic *reidh* (ray), a flat space of land, as Raeclòch near Turriff—*reidh cloich*, stone flat; Raemòir in Moray and Aberdeenshire—*reidh mór*, great flat.

Gaelic *boc* is now usually restricted in meaning to a he-goat, but its radical signification seems to be a male animal, in the same sense as we say a "buck" rabbit, and it often stands for the roebuck, which is probably the true meaning in Glenbùck, Lanarkshire. But in Teutonic names it means the male fallow-deer, as Bùckhurst in Lanarkshire—O.N.E. *bucce hurst*, buck-wood; Bùxburn in Aberdeenshire being the buck's burn. Buccleùch is usually interpreted buck's cleugh or ravine, and in the neighbourhood "cleugh" enters freely into place-names, such as Harecleuch, Gilbertscleugh, Windycleuch, &c.; but I cannot indorse this interpretation, to bear which the name *must* be sounded Bùccleuch. It is probably a corruption of some Gaelic name, with the

Their Lesson. 123

stress on the last syllable, which has been altered in spelling to suit the supposed meaning.

Besides the domestic pig, which was in early use among the people, the wild swine was a favourite beast of chase all over Scotland. No animal has left its name so commonly impressed on the topography, and it is seldom easy to distinguish between the wild and domestic beasts. *Torc*, a boar, was the origin of Drumtùrk in Perthshire and Glentùrk in Wigtownshire, from the genitive singular *tuirc;* and Mindòrk in the latter county is *moine torc*, the moor of the boars, from the genitive plural *torc*.

<small>Swine.</small>

The Anglo-Saxon for "boar" was *bár*, whence Beàrsden, near Glasgow; but Bòrland or Bòreland, a name given forty-one times in the Postal Directory, means a home farm—land kept for the "board" of the laird's house. Bòrestone, again, in many places, means a stone which has been pierced, a name which must yield in antiquity to Thìrlestane in Selkirkshire and Berwickshire, from A.S. þirlian, to pierce.

Countless are the names from *muc*, a sow, which has also become the generic name for swine. Clachanamùck in Wigtownshire is *clachan nam muc*, stones of the swine. Drummùck, near Girvan, is the swine-ridge, a name which by umlaut becomes Swìndridge, near Dalry, in the same county, and Swìnhill in Lanarkshire. Even so, Balmùick, near Crieff, *baile muic*, swine-farm, appears in Anglo-Saxon as Swìnton in Berwickshire and near Glasgow. There is a place near Greenock curiously named Lemnamùick, which signifies *leum na muic*, the sow's leap.

Ben Macdhùi, as we choose to write the mountain of that name, is usually interpreted *beinn muic duibhe*, hill of the black sow; but Highlanders call it *Beinn-a'-boch-duibh*, hill of the black goat. The Muck, a tributary of the Ayrshire Stinchar, was originally *amhuinn muc*, sow's river.

A swine-pasture or haunt of swine is *muclach* or *mucreach*, producing Glenamùckloch in Argyleshire, Drummùckloch in Galloway, and so in many other counties, and Mùckrach, near Grantown-on-Spey.

Wild cattle.

Places named after cattle lie under the same uncertainty as those named after swine; we do not know whether the wild or the domesticated animal is referred to. The Caledonian bull was a formidable animal, as may be realised by contemplating, at a safe distance, his lineal descendants in Cadzow Forest and at Chillingham in Northumberland. The Gaelic word for bull is *tarbh* (tarriv), doubtless akin to Latin *taurus*, and becoming in Welsh *taru*, in Cornish *tarow*, and in Manx *tarroo*. Knockentàrry in Wigtownshire is doubtless *cnoc an tairbhe*, the bull's hill; but Knockenhàrry, a name occurring in many places, is *cnoc an fhaire* (harry), hill of the watching.

The Tarf is the name of different streams in Perthshire, Inverness-shire, Forfarshire, Kirkcudbright, and Wigtownshire, and the Tarth in Peeblesshire is the same name, all named from bulls; not, as has been

Their Lesson.

elaborately propounded, because of their roaring noise,—it never would suggest itself to the natural man to put such a strain on the imagination. Besides, the Peeblesshire Tarth happens to be a peculiarly sluggish stream. The name arose from some forgotten circumstance of hunting or pastoral life; the original name in each case would be *amhuinn tarbh*, bull's stream.

Damh (dav), an ox, is preserved in Dalnadàmph, land of the oxen; in Blairdàff in Aberdeenshire—*blár damh*, ox-field; and Inchnadàmph in Sutherlandshire —*inis na' damh*, ox-pasture.

Bo, a cow, cognate with Latin *bos*, may easily be recognised in Drumbòw in Lanarkshire, the cow's ridge, and in Achnabà, twice in Argyleshire, the cow-field. In Galloway strips of seaside pasture sometimes bear the name of Scràbba or Scràbbie. This name must be added to Tiree as an unusual instance of the movement of stress from the specific to the generic syllable. It is the same name as Scrabo, near Newtonards in Ireland—that is, *scrath bo*, cow's grass, from *scrath* (scraw), sward. Bòwling on the Clyde takes its name from a stream—*bo linn*, cow's pool.

Laogh (leuh), a calf, is usually contracted into the termination -lay or -lee, and is thus liable to be confused with *liath* (lee), grey. Barlàe occurs six or seven times in Galloway, and has the same meaning as Càwvis Hill, just outside the burgh of Wigtown. Other forms are Barlaùgh in Ayrshire, Auchlèach in Wigtownshire, Auchlày in Sutherland, Auchlèe in Aberdeenshire, and Drumlèy in Galloway and Ayrshire. Craiglèy in Urr parish, Kirkcudbright, is probably *creag laogh*, the calves' crag; but Craiglèe, overlooking Loch Trool in the same county, is more likely to be *creag liath*, grey crag. Ballochalèe, a ford on the Wigtownshire Tarf, may be interpreted *bealach na' laogh*, pass of the calves. All are to be distinguished by the position of the stress from the Anglo-Saxon *lea*, a field, in such common names as Whìtelee, Bròwnlee, Yèllowlee, wherein the terminal -lee is the generic syllable.

The wolf. The most formidable beast of prey in the old forest was, of course, the wolf, and we might expect to find frequent reference to it among place-names; but it is not easy to identify it with certainty.

It was called by various names—*madadh, allaidh, bréach, faol*, and *mactire* or son of the soil. Now there is no more familiar termination of place-names than -maddie or -moddie—such as Drummòddie, *druim madadh* (madduh), wolf-ridge; Blairmòddie, *blár madadh*, wolf-field; Claymòddie, formerly Glenmaddie, *gleann madadh*, wolf-glen—all in Wigtownshire; and Culmàddie, *cuil madadh*, wolf's corner, in Sutherlandshire. These represent the two extremities of Scotland, and the word occurs frequently between those limits; but the strict meaning of *madadh* is a dog, and *madadh ruadh* means a fox. But the commoner words for dog and fox are *cu*, gen. *con*, and *sionach* (shinnagh), and it is almost certain that *madadh* in place-names generally means a wolf.

Bréach is an obsolete word for wolf, which cannot be distinguished now from *breac*, piebald, brindled, a term often applied to land; but probably it survives in Tarbrèoch in Kirkcudbrightshire—*tìr bréach*, wolf-ground; and Killibràkes, Wigtownshire, is perhaps *coille bréach*, wolf-wood. Bràco in Perthshire and Aberdeenshire may be compared with Breagho in Fermanagh, which the Irish Annalists used to write Bréagh mhagh (vah), wolf-field.

Wòlflee, near Hawick, is the Anglo-Saxon equivalent of Blairmòddie; Wòlfhill, near Perth, of Drummòddie; and Wòlf-cleuch, near St Mary's Loch, of Glenmàddy. Ulbster in Caithness, Ulsta in Shetland, and Wòlfstar in East Lothian are probably named from men called Ulf — *Ulfr bólstaðr*, Ulf's farm.

Cu, a dog, gen. *con*, enters freely into place-names, but it was also a favourite name among men. Thus Loch Conn in Perthshire, reflecting the name of Lough Conn in Mayo, may either be Conn's lake or dog's lake; but Achnacòne in Appin is clearly *achadh na' con*, field of dogs, because of the article. Aspirated as *chon*, this is probably the origin of many names ending in -quhan — as Boqohàn in Stirlingshire, *both Chon*, Conn's hut; Blairqohàn in Ayrshire, Conn's or the dog's field; Killiewhàn in Kirkcudbrightshire—*coille chon*, wood of the dogs. *Gadhar* or *gaothar* (gaiur), a greyhound, from *gaeth*

The dog.

(geu), the wind, in allusion to its swiftness, yields Glengỳre in Wigtownshire.

The wild cat. The wild cat, now wellnigh extinct, is commonly mentioned in the place-names of all three languages. Thus in Gaelic there is Craigencàt in many counties, the wild cat's crag; Lingàt in Wigtownshire, *linn cat*, the wild cat's linn; Auchnagàtt, a station on the Great North of Scotland Railway in Aberdeenshire, field of the wild cats. So in Saxon speech we find Càtscleugh, near Denny; Càtshaw in Roxburghshire, the wild cat's wood; Càtslack in Selkirkshire, the wild cat's gap; and in Norse such names as Càttadale, near Campbeltown, the wild cat's dale, and Càtgill, near Cànonbie, in Dumfriesshire, the wild cat's ravine.

The otter. *Dorán*, the otter—*i.e., dobhuran*, the water-beast—produces Glendòwran in Lanarkshire; Aldòuran in Wigtownshire—*allt doran*, otter-stream, like Otterbourne in Northumberland; Puldòuran in Kirkcudbright, with the same meaning; and Craigendòran in Dumbartonshire, *creag an dorain*, the otter's rock, or *creagean doran*, rocks of the otters.

The badger. *Broc*, a badger, derived, like *breac*, a trout, from *breac*, parti-coloured, was borrowed from the Gaelic by the Anglo-Saxon, and forms many land-names in both languages. These remain in many places where badgers are no longer found. Thus Bròckloch, the name of several places in Ayrshire, is simply the Gaelic *broclach*, a badger-warren, while Bròcklees in the same county is the Saxon for badger-field;

Bròcket in Ayrshire and Lanarkshire is *brocc wudu*, badger-wood. Bròckwoodlees in Dumfriesshire shows fields named from a badger-wood, and Bròxburn in Linlithgowshire is the badger's stream. The Gaelic equivalent of Bròcket comes out as Kilbròcks, near Stranraer — *coill broc*, badger-wood; and from the genitive singular, *bruic*, come Kilbròok, near Moffat —*coill bruic*, badger-wood; and Auchabrìck in Wigtownshire—*achadh bruic*, badger-field.

I have only identified one Gaelic place-name commemorating another of our fauna now wellnigh extinct, the polecat or foumart—viz., Corriefècklach in the Galloway hills, *coire feocalach*, foumart's corrie.

The polecat.

LECTURE VI.

THE LESSON OF PLACE-NAMES.

THE LAND—ITS SURFACE AND DIVISIONS—OPEN LAND INSEPARABLE FROM THE IDEA OF FIGHTING—NORSE PENNYLANDS—OCCUPATIONS AND TRADES — CRIME AND PUNISHMENT — POVERTY—DISEASE—RIVERS AND STREAMS—ECCLESIASTICAL NAMES—EARLY DEDICATIONS OF CHAPELS AND WELLS—PRIESTS AND MONKS—LAND NOT USUALLY NAMED BY THE EARLY CELTS FROM OWNERSHIP—BUT FREQUENTLY SO BY TEUTONIC PEOPLE — LAND-NAMES GIVEN TO MEN — MEN'S NAMES GIVEN TO LANDS—CONCLUSION.

T will tax all my ingenuity to compress within the limits of a single hour all the subjects set forth in the syllabus to be dealt with in this, the last lecture of the course. In order to do so with any prospect of usefulness, I propose to take the Gaelic, as the characteristic language of North Britain, noticing a few synonyms in the other languages which we have already considered.

The land.   The Gaelic word most nearly corresponding to English "land" or "ground" is *tir*. It is allied to

Latin *terra*, and comes from a root signifying "dry." It is the same in Irish and Welsh, but forms no part of Manx place-names. The island of Tiree is called by Adamnan Terra Ethica, as if named from Ith, the legendary uncle of the Irish hero Miledh. But it is more probably *tir idhe*, corn-land, from an old Gaelic word *iodh*, corn; for it is a fertile island, " callit in all tymes M'Connells [Macdonald's] girnel." Tirfèrgus, near Campbeltown, Fergus's land, corresponds to Tiràrgus in Donegal, where the *f* is aspirated to silence—*tir Fhearguis*. Tardòw in Wigtownshire is probably *tir dubh*, black ground; but Tarwilkie or Tirwilkie in Kirkcudbright is *treabh giolcach*, rushy farm, for in 1604 it is spelt Tragilhey; and Terrègles in Dumfriesshire, commonly interpreted *tir eglais*, is really *treamhar eglais*, being spelt Travereglis in a charter of David II.

Tinlùskie in Wigtownshire is *tir loisgthe* (luskie), burnt land, by the common interchange of *r* and *n*, corresponding to the frequent Anglo-Saxon names Bruntland, Brunthill, and Bruntisfield.

As a suffix *tir* is found in Cantỳre or Kintỳre, the head or end of the land, just as Kintàil is *cinn t-shael* (tale), head of the tide, and Kinvàrra—*cinn mhara*, head of the sea. Glàister and Glàisters in Ayrshire, Arran, Kirkcudbright, Lanark, and Glàster Law near Arbroath, are *glas tir*, green land; and in Glàsserton Fell in Wigtownshire there is a curious example of the A.S. *tun* and the Norse *fjal* added to the Gaelic *glas thir* (glassir) or *glas ghart* (glass art), green paddock.

Scottish Land-Names.

Fields.   *Magh*, a plain, rendered by Latin writers *campus* and *planities*, has fallen out of use in modern Gaelic; but its derivative, *machair* or *machaire*, with a strong instead of a weak guttural, is still used to denote flat land near the sea. *Magh* appears as Moy, near Inverness, Fort-William, Forres, Beauly, and Campbeltown; as Mye in Wigtownshire and Stirlingshire. A still older form of the word—*mag*—is preserved in Mùgdock, in Dumbartonshire, where in 750 there was a battle between the Britons and the Picts of Manann, and Talorgan, the Pictish leader, was slain. It is written Magedauc and Mogetauc in the Cambrian Annals.

As a suffix, *magh* is liable to aspiration, and the *m* disappears, as in Mòrrach twice in Wigtownshire —*mur mhagh*, land overlooking the sea. This also may be regarded as the origin of the name Mòray, anciently spelt Muref, and latinised Moravia. The change of *gh* into *f* is shown in Muff, corrupted from *magh*, the name of several places in the north of Ireland. In that country *mur-mhagh*, so written by the Four Masters, but which Cormac disguised as *murbhach*, has become Mùrvagh in Donegal, Mùrrow in Wicklow (very like our Mòray), and Mùrvey, Mùrragh, Mùrroo, and Mùrreagh in other counties. The same compound, *mooragh*, means a sandbank in the Isle of Man.

Machair, supposed to be *magh thír*, plain land, is so common in our place-names as to require little notice, except to observe that the parishes of Old and New Machar, in Aberdeen, commemorate a dedication to St Machorius. But there are two farms near Stranraer in which the stress serves to distinguish the meanings of two very similar names. One is Màcher, which is simply *machair*, a plain. It is part of the great plain lying between the two divisions of Wigtownshire, the Machers on the east and the Rhinns on the west. The other is Mahàar, signifying either *magh air*, east field, or the field of the ploughing or of the slaughter—for in old as in modern Gaelic, *àr* bears either meaning.

Màchrie, near Ardrossan, represents the third form, *machaire* (maghery).

Of all Celtic names descriptive of occupied land, none are so common in Scotland as *achadh* (aha) and *baile* (bally). Pont explains *achadh* as "ane Irich vord signifying a folde or a crofte of land gained out of a vylde ground of before vnmanured." Adamnan translates it "campulus," and it corresponds most nearly to our word "field."

As a prefix it appears as Acha, Achy, Auch, and, with the article, Auchen and Achna. Achnacàrry, the seat of Lochiel on the Arkaig, takes its name from a disused fishery—*achadh na coraidh*, field of the weir.

The surname Afflèck, taken from places of that name in Aberdeenshire, is a shortened form of Auchinlèck in Ayrshire, Lanark, and Forfar—*achadh na leac*, field of the flagstones.

Gàrioch, a district in Aberdeenshire, represents *garbh achadh* or *garbh mhach*, as may be seen in old writings, in which it appears as Garuiauche, *c.* 1170; Garvyach, *c.* 1180; and Garviagha, *c.* 1297. Gàrwachy in Wigtownshire and Gàrvock in Kincardineshire are the same compound.

Àrdoch, in Perthshire and many other counties, is plainly *ard mhagh,* or *ard achadh,* high field; but Ardàchy, in Wigtownshire, is shown by the stress to be *ard achaidh,* hill of the cultivated field—a very natural name in a district where cultivation was rare.

Baile, a farm, homestead, or village, so exactly corresponds to A.S. *tún* and Norse *by, bær,* or *bólstaðr,* and is so easily recognised in composition, that I need not dwell on it further than to say it is glossed *locus* in the 'Book of Armagh' and other ancient MSS. Dr Reeves says that in Ireland 6400 townlands begin with Bal or Bally, upwards of one-tenth of the whole. As a suffix, *baile* borrows the disguise of the aspirate, as Shanvàlley and Shinvòllie in Galloway—*sean bhaile* (vally), old place; but Loch Vàlley in Galloway, like Meal-na-bhealaich in Perthshire, is *loch bhealaich* (vallah), loch of the pass.

Blár in modern Gaelic means a battle, but its primary meaning is a plain. It is unknown in the topography of Ireland, Wales, Man, Cornwall, and Brittany, and its distribution in Scotland is somewhat peculiar. It is pretty common, both singly and in composition, from Galloway on the south-west, through Strathclyde, Stirling, Perth, Forfar, Fife, and Aberdeen. It is found in Arran, Dumbarton, as Blairhòsh—*blár shuas* (hosh), upper field, Blairnàirn—*blár n' fhearn*, alder-field, but not in Argyleshire or the Isles, nor in the Border counties from Dumfries eastward. The solitary occurrence in the Lothians of Blaircòchrane sounds suspiciously like a modern importation. It only occurs once in Inverness, and once in the east of Ross-shire. Furthest north, in Sutherland, there is Blairninìch—*blár nan each*, field of the horses.

Its use, therefore, is confined to a strip of country running from south-west to north-east; but it is not easy to found any ethnological conclusion thereon, because this strip includes the territories of the Niduarian Picts, the Britons of Strathclyde, the Picts of Manann, and the Northern Picts. That the usual meaning is a field and not a battle seems clear from the occurrence of Blairshìnnoch—*blár sionach* (shinnagh), fox-field, in counties so far apart as Wigtownshire and Banff. The Old Northern English equivalent to Blairshìnnoch is Tòdley, near Whithorn, and Tòdholm, near Paisley.

That excellent Celtic scholar, Professor Mackinnon, in discussing this word, falls into the snare which seems to beset every one who takes up Gaelic lore, as if the Celtic race were unlike the rest of mankind. "Is there any country in the world," he asks, "except the Highlands of Scotland, where the common word for a flat piece of ground, *blár*, has come to mean a battle-field?" Undoubtedly there is. The Latin *campus*, a field, assumed in Low Latin the special meaning of "a duel, battle, war." Thence, through the French, comes our "camp," which in Middle English never bore the modern restricted meaning of a "tented field," but meant a battle. In Anglo-Saxon *camp* was a battle, *campsted* a battle-field, the latter of which is the origin of our place-name, Càmpsie, near Glasgow, Perth, and Kirriemuir. Champain, open country, and campaign are twin words. A.S. *cempa*, N. *kempa*, a champion, one who holds the field, and *field* exercise, *field*-marshal, a *park* of artillery, are other examples of the intimate association, in Teutonic as well as in Celtic minds, of open space with fighting.

So let us dismiss for ever, if we want to arrive at the real significance of Celtic place-names, all idea that the Gael was more valiant, more pugnacious, or more poetic than other people.

Fearann, a derivative of *fear*, a man, described land in the occupation of a man, as Ferintòsh in Moray—*fearann toisich*, thane's land; but it very often took the aspirate, and becoming *fhearann*, was written *earrann*. We find some curious groups of holdings thus designated. In Stirlingshire there are Arnprìor, Arngìbbon, Arnfìnlay, and others adjacent. In Kirkcudbright there are Ernàmbrie; Ernànity— *earrann annuid*, church-land; Ernèspie, *earrann espuig*, bishop's land; Ernfìllan, Fillan's land; Ernminzie—all in Crossmichael parish. Now *airn* is Broad Scots for "iron," hence in the same county the names occur of Ironhàsh, Ironlòsh (1456, Arnglosh)—*earrann loise*, burnt land; Ironmacànnie

(1512, Erne Macanny), Ironmànnoch—*earrann manach*, monk's land; Irongrày (1466, Yrngray), *earrann graich*, land of the horse-drove, for this was the province where the Galloway nags were bred.

Gort or *gart*, an enclosure or paddock, is a Gaelic word of very wide affinity. It is closely cognate with Norse *garðr* and English "yard," "garth," "garden," which own a common descent with the Latin *hortus*.

Garth, near Lerwick, is certainly Norse, like almost all place-names in Shetland; but Garth in Perthshire and Forfar is either Old Northern English or, like the Gart in the former county, Gaelic. Balnòwlart, in South Ayrshire, is a curious contraction of *baile n' ubhal ghart* (owlhart), apple-yard farm; and Airiequhillart in Wigtownshire is *airidh ubhal ghart* (airy owlhart), shieling of the apple-yard, having its Norse equivalents in Appleby in the same county — *epla by*, and Àpplegarth, a parish in Annandale, a district rich in Norse names — *epla garðr*. But Applecròss in Ross-shire, where St Maelrubha founded a church in 673, is known to have been Aber Crossain, mouth of the Crossan water.

Dùart in Argyleshire and Perthshire is *dubh ghart* (doo hart), black paddock; and the Glàssert near Aberfoyle, and Glàzert in Ayrshire, are *glas ghart* (hart), green paddock. Among other examples may be cited Gartnanìch in Stirlingshire—*gart nan each* (aigh), horse-paddock; Gartclòss in Stirlingshire and Gartclùsh in Lanarkshire—*gart clois*, paddock of the trench; Gartwhìnnie in Stirlingshire—*gart fheannagh,* enclosure of the lazy-beds; Gartùrk in Lanarkshire — *gart tuirc,* boar's paddock; Gartshèrrie in Lanarkshire — *gart searrach,* paddock of the colts; and Gortinanàne in Cantyre—*gortin nan én,* enclosure of the birds.

Garadh is a garden, and takes the same form as *garbh* (garriv), rough, in composition. Thus the river Garry is *amhuinn garbh,* a word which in other streams has become Yarrow in Selkirkshire and Gryfe in Renfrewshire. But in an old estate-map of Cuil, Kirkcudbright, I found a number of plots near a village marked with such names as Garriefàd, Garrieslàe, and Garrienàe, alongside of others designated M'Kie's Garden, Peggy Murray's Garden, &c.

Mountains and hills.

Gaelic names for hill and dale form a long list, of which time will permit no more than a very brief survey.

Beinn (ben) is the commonest term for a mountain in the Highlands, forming the prefix of innumerable names; but as a suffix it is generally altered by the aspirate, as in Gùlvain in Inverness-shire—*gabhal bheinn* (gowl ven), fork of the hill.

Some Gaelic philologists draw a distinction in spelling between *beinn,* a hill, and *beann,* a corner or point, but they represent the same root.

Beannach means horned, and the English "horn" and "corner" are both closely connected with the Latin *cornu,* a horn, showing the same mental process at work in producing similar groups of words in widely different languages.

In the sense of a horn, *beinn* naturally became descriptive of a steep hill. In Ireland it is more generally applied to small hills. It does not occur among the mountains of Man, though some high land near the coast is called Binnbuie, corresponding to Benbòwie Craigs on the coast of Glasserton in Wigtownshire—*beinn buidhe*, yellow horn or headland. In the former case the epithet *buidhe* is earned by the flower of gorse, in the latter by the yellow lichen which still stains the sea-cliff, as it did when the name was conferred centuries ago.

In the mountain-ranges of Galloway *beinn* occurs rather sparingly in the names of high hills: *e.g.*, Benyèllary (2359 feet)—*beinn iolaire* (yillary), eagle's hill; and Bengrày (1175 feet)—*beinn gréaich*, hill of the high flat, or *graich*, of the horse-drove. But it is not confined to hills, for an isolated pointed rock in the tideway of the coast of Kirkmaiden, Wigtownshire, is known as Bennùskie—*beinn uisce*, the "ben" or horn in the water.

More common in Galloway is the derivative *beinnán*, either singly, as the Bènnan, or in composition, as Bennanbràck—*beinnán breac*, dappled hill.

The adjectival form *beinnach*, which in Ireland gives such names as Bannaghbane and Bannaghroe, the white and the red hilly ground, appears in Scotland as Craigbènnoch in Wigtownshire, horned crag, and as Bènny, near Braco, in Perthshire. The most ancient examples of this word *beinnach* occurring in literature, with the proper indication of the quantity of the Celtic termination—ācus (*āco-s*)—are, as M. de Joubainville has pointed out, contained in two lines of Virgil :—

"Fluctibus et fremitu assurgens, Benāce, marino."
—*Georg.*, ii. 160.
"Quos patre Benāco, velatus arundine longa."
—*Æn.*, x. 205.

Benacus is here the name given to the Lac de Garde, in Cisalpine Gaul, and occurs twice in the poetry of Claudian :—

"Quas Benācus alit, quas excipit amne quieto Mincius."
—*Epith. Pall. et Cel.*, 107.
"Benācumque putat littora rubra lacum."
—*Carmina*, xiii. 18.

This suffix—ach (originally āco-s)—is reduced to a single consonant in the name York—Eboracus, the place of Eburus.

Cnoc, commonest of all Gaelic names for a hill, has already been dealt with, and it has been shown how, in districts where Gaelic is still spoken, the pronunciation has been altered to *crochd*. In Anglicised counties it is easily recognised, though its meaning has been entirely forgotten, as is shown by the common pleonasm Knock Hill. Knockhilly, however, the name of a place near Southwick in Kirkcudbright, is not such an absurd name as it looks, for it is *cnoc chuille* (hwilly), wood hill. Cùmnock, in Ayrshire, represents *cam cnoc*, bent hill.

Though *cnoc* occurs several times on the map of Dumfriesshire, it has almost disappeared in the eastern lowlands under the influence of English nomenclature; but the Knock, a farm name near Duns, in Berwickshire, shows that it was once well established there.

Sliabh (slieve or slew) is glossed *mons* in the Zeuss MSS., but in Scotland it bears the significance of a moorland rather than a mountain. It may be traced in Berwickshire in the name Sligh, near Edrom, which is nearly the same in form as Sliagh in the parish of Drumblàde, Aberdeenshire, where Bruce had an encampment in 1307, and successfully resisted the forces of Comyn.

Slamànnan in Stirlingshire is *sliabh Manann,* the moor of the Manann Picts; Slayhòrrie is a village near Nairn—*sliabh choire,* moor of the caldron or corrie; and in Wigtownshire this word forms the prefix of about thirty names, as Slewsmìrroch—*sliabh smeurach,* blackberry moor; Slewcàirn—*sliabh carn,* moor of the cairns, like Slieve Carna in Ireland; Slaehàrbrie—*sliabh Chairbre,* Cairbre's moor, which is the same as Slieve Carbury, in County Longford.

The plural *sleibhte* (slatey) gives its name to Sleat, in Skye, where the word seems to bear its original meaning of "hills," for that parish is bisected by a range rising to a height of 2400 feet. But the Slate Islands, off the coast of Lorn, have received an English name from the roofing-slate which they produce.

Druim, a back, a ridge, is supposed to be cognate with the Latin *dorsum*.

Early as Anglian speech was established, and long as it has been spoken to the exclusion of all other, in the Lothians, it has not prevailed to extirpate this word, most characteristic of Gaelic topography. Drum may be found singly upwards of thirty times in the Postal Directory of Scotland. Within easy reach of Edinburgh there is Drum at Liberton, Drem in East Lothian, and Drummòre at Musselburgh. The last-mentioned name, sometimes written Dromòre, is very common in Scotland and Ireland, and appears near Lochgilphead with the aspirate— Drumvòre.

From Roxburgh and Berwick shires it has disappeared, but all over the west, north, and central parts of Scotland it is universal and easily recognised.

The plural nominative *dromán* comes out as Drỳmen, in Stirlingshire; and the genitive singular *droma* gives Kildrùmmie, a high-lying parish in Aberdeen, which means either *cil, coill*, or *cúl droma*, the church, the wood, or the back of the ridge. Loch Dròma in Ross-shire, the lake of the ridge, is so named from its position on the central ridge or backbone of Scotland.

This word *druim* seems to have suggested Ptolemy's Καληδόνιος δρυμός. It is as characteristic of Irish and Manx as of Scottish topography, but the Welsh equivalent *trum* is much more sparingly used.

Meall (myall), a lump or nob, O. Erse *mell*, perhaps akin to Latin *moles*, is a very common hill-name in Gaelic districts. A special favourite in Sutherland, it is spread all over the Highlands, and reappears in the mountainous region of Galloway, where it generally assumes the form Mill in composition. Thus Millhàrry—*meall fhaire* (harry), the watch-hill—and Millmòre, in Kirkcudbright, have the same prefix as Mealgàrve in Sutherland—*meall garbh*, rough hill, and Mealmòre in Inverness—*meall mór*, great hill. Sometimes it appears in Anglian disguise even in the Highlands, and Millifiàch, near Beauly, is not to be recognised at first sight as *meall a' fithiaich*, hill of the raven. Milnàb, near Crieff, is the abbot's hill; Milmànnoch, near Ayr, the monk's hill; and Miljòan, near Girvan, *meall don*, brown hill.

Mael (moyle), bald, bare, is a different word from the last, though not easily to be distinguished from it in place-names, especially as it is used to denote hills and headlands on account of their baldness or bareness. It is found in all Celtic dialects, in Welsh *moel*, in Breton *môal*, and, entering into personal names, implied service, from shaving the head being a sign of slavery.[1] Malcolm is *mael Coluim*, Col-

---

[1] The obligation to shave, which, even in our own day, rests upon soldiers and domestic servants, may be traced to the primitive custom of mutilating prisoners of war, who were made slaves. The tonsure of priests is part of the same tradition: they are *celi Dé*—servants of God. The Mosaic law tempered the severity of mutilation by the instructions for re-engaging a servant set forth in

umba's bald (servant), Milroy *mael Ruarich*, Rory's servant. Besides confusion with *meall, mael* is practically often indistinguishable from the Norse *múli*, a snout, which also expresses a peak or promontory. Thus the Mull of Cantyre in Gaelic is *Mael Cintire*, but *Satiris múli* in the Sagas. The natives always talk of the Mull of Galloway as the Moyle, which points to a Gaelic origin, corresponding to the many places called Moyle in various parts of Ireland.

Mullach, mullán, and *mollachan* are derivatives of *mael*, as *beinnach* and *beinnán* are of *beinn*. The first forms the name of Mùllach in Aberdeenshire, Kirkcudbright, and Wigtownshire, and Mullochàrd, near Aviemore, in Inverness-shire, *mullach ard*, high bare place. The second gives Mòllance in Kirkcudbright, Mòllands near Callander, Mòlland in Stirlingshire, Mùllion near Perth, Mòllin near Lockerby, and Mollandhù near Dumbarton—*mullán dubh*, black hill; while to *mollachan* may be traced Millegan, in Banff.

Barr, the end, top, or tip of anything, hence, in topography, a hill-top.[1] The basal meaning of the word is probably connected with A.S. *bær*, bare,

---

Exodus xxi. 6: "Then his master shall bring him unto the judges; he shall also bring him to the door, or unto the door-post; and his master shall bore his ear through with an awl; and he shall serve him for ever." As civilisation advanced, the code became milder, and was fulfilled, even in the case of convicts, by shaving the hair.

[1] In modern Gaelic *barr* means crop, the crop on the ground, —probably from corn growing best, in the absence of draining, on the dry hill-tops.

so its application to a hill-top is equivalent to *mael.* It is of sparing occurrence in Ireland, and in Scotland it is confined to the western and southwestern counties. Out of about 500 Celtic names beginning with Bar in the Postal Directory, only two or three are in the east, such as Barhill near Fochabers, and Barflat near Rhynie in Aberdeenshire, and it is not certain that these are Celtic. But all through the west, Bar is nearly as frequent as Knock and Drum, with much the same meaning.

When the prefix *bar* is followed by the article in the feminine genitive singular or genitive plural, it gives a form indistinguishable from *bearna* (barna), a cleft or passage between two hills. Thus Barnecàllagh in Wigtownshire and Barncàlzie in Kirkcudbright are probably *barr na cailleaich,* hill-top of the woman, witch, or nun; Barnamòn in Wigtownshire, *barr nam ban,* hill-top of the women (like Cornamon in Cavan and Leitrim); but Barneywàter in the mountain district of Kirkcudbright is a corruption of *bearna uachdar,* upper pass.

As a suffix in the genitive, *barr* takes the aspirate, as in the well-known name of Lochinvàr, in Kirkcudbright—*loch an bharra,* lake of the hill.

Monadh (munny), a moor, is the same as the Welsh *mynydd,* a mountain, Bret. and Cornish *monedh.* Dr Joyce interprets the Irish *muine* (munny), a shrubbery or brake, but says it is sometimes applied to hills. It is no doubt the

K

same word used in the sense of a "waste." The modern Gaelic *moine* (mōny), peat or morass, is another form of it; and in place-names beginning Mon-, Mony-, Munny-, or Minnie-, the precise meaning can only be ascertained by examining the locality. *Monadh* gives their name to the Mùnnock hills in Ayrshire. Moncrìeff is spelt Monidcroib and Monagh craebe — *monadh craebh*, moor of the trees—in the Annals of Tighernac, who, writing in the eleventh century, records a battle at that place in the year 728 between two forces of Picts, in which Angus obtained a victory over Alpin.[1]

Mentèith, anciently spelt Meneted and Menetethe, is the moor of the river Teith.[2] The word is also perpetuated in the well-known range formerly called The Mounth, which, traversing Scotland from Ben Nevis on the west to the Monadhliath on the east, was also known as Drumalban, or the backbone of Scotland. The pass which leads across this range from the Mearns is still called Cairn o' Mount, and appears as Monitcarno in the Annals of Ulster and Mynyd Carno in the Welsh Bruts.

Other instances are Moniemòre in Arran, the great moor; Monybùie in Kirkcudbright, yellow moor; Monygùile in Arran — *monadh goill*, the stranger's moor.

Ard or *aird*, a height, from the same root as

---

[1] Chronicles of the Picts and Scots, p. 74.
[2] *De situ Albanie*, Colbertine MS., twelfth century.

the Latin *arduus*, is the substantival adjective *ard*—steep, high—and forms a very familiar syllable in Scottish place-names. Some of the best known are Ardrìshaig—*ard driseag*, thorny height; Ardentìnny—*ard an teine*, beacon height; Ardròssan—*ard rosain*, height of the little headland. Not unfrequently it stands alone, when it generally receives the English plural [1] and becomes Airds, a name found repeatedly in Perthshire, Argyleshire, Galloway, and Ayrshire. But in the north it often becomes Ord, as the Ord of Caithness; and, in the south, Ornòckenoch in Kirkcudbright is *ard cnocnach*, height of the knolls.

Braigh, a top or summit, forms part of many names, as Braemòre in Ross-shire and Caithness, but it is not always to be distinguished from Broad Scots "brae," which probably comes from the same root. *Braigh* remains, with little change, as Breich, a station on the Caledonian Railway between Edinburgh and Glasgow. In Ireland it is written *bri* or *bré*, and gives a name to various places called Bray, thus proving it to have been used in Gaelic independently of Anglian influence; but the in-

---

[1] It is not always clear whether *s* at the end of Anglicised Celtic names (generally monosyllables) is the English plural or possessive singular. It is the practice in Scotland to call a landowner or tenant after the name of his land. Thus the tenant of Aird is known as Aird, and his dwelling-place becomes known as Aird's (house). Sometimes the *s* is added from analogy or euphemism. Thus Lord Stair is commonly spoken of by the peasantry as Lord Stairs.

numerable Braeheads and Braesides in our land have no direct connection with Celtic speech.

The old Erse was *brage,* from the genitive case of which, *bragat,* springs the word *braghad* (braad), the neck, which has a double significance. It may either mean the throat, and be applied in topography to a gorge[1] or narrow glen, or the breast when it denotes a swelling upland.[2] In the latter sense it gives their name to the Braid Hills, near Edinburgh; and Breadàlban means the breast or upland of Alban or Scotland. But in Galloway there are gullies on the sea-coast bearing the name Bràdock and Brèddock, which have the meaning of *braghadach,* a throat-like place.

Another Gaelic word, *brù* or *bruach,* a bank, mound, acclivity, is the equivalent to our expression the "brow" of a hill, and the terms are probably cognate. It will be observed that in Broad Scots the same distinction is preserved between "brae" and "brow" as there is in Gaelic between *braigh* and *bruach,* although both signify rising land. A Scotsman speaks of a "brae-face" and the "broo o' the hill." It is, however, impossible to distinguish *bruach* in place-names from *brugh,* a house, one of the forms assumed by the old Irish *borg, brog.* Brough and Brough Hill, in Galloway, may represent either word. The latter was written Burgh

---

[1] The words "gorge" and "gully," both synonyms of "throat," bear a similar figurative application to a narrow glen or channel.

[2] So we speak of "breasting" a hill, and of a "breastwork."

Jerg and Brugh jarg in Inquisitions of the seventeenth century, corresponding to Brougderg in Cavan, Fermanagh, and Tyrone.

Learg (larg), a slope or hillside, is the name of many places in Scotland, Ireland, and Man. Lairg in Sutherlandshire, Larg in Galloway (generally the Larg), Largue in Aberdeenshire, and Lurg near Crieff and again near Fintry, are instances of it; and Largs on the Clyde has the English plural added. Larbràx in Wigtownshire is given in Pont's map as Lairgbrecks and Lairgbrecks Gressy—*learg breac greusaich*, the cobbler's dappled hillside.

A commoner form of the word is *leargaidh* (largie), becoming Làrgo in Fife, Làrgie in Ayrshire and Aberdeenshire, Largiemòre and Largiebèg in Arran, the great and the little hillside; Largiebrèak, the deer forest in Jura—*leargaidh breac*, brindled hillside; and Largiewèe in Wigtownshire — *leargaidh bhuidh* (wee), yellow hillside.

Another derivative of *learg* is *leargán* (largan), which produces Lùrgan near Aberfeldy, a name which, in Ireland, gives his title to Lord Lurgan, literally lord of the hillside.

Another name for a hillside, generally a wet one, is *leitir* (letter), which Cormac (whose etymology, however, is not to be relied on) derives from *leth tirim agus leth fliuch*, half dry and half wet. It is more likely *leth tír*, half land, from the side being, as it were, half the hill. It is the source of many names, as Lètter, farms in the counties of Aberdeen,

Dumbarton, Stirling, and Perth. In composition it appears in Lettermòre, great hillside, in Argyleshire; Letterbèg, little hillside, in Aberdeenshire; and Letterdhù, dark hillside, in Perthshire.

The plural *latracha* gives Lèttrick near Glasgow, and Làthro near Wick.

In the southern counties the only instance of this word known to me is Letterpìn, near Girvan.

Cruach, a stack of corn or peats, is sometimes used to denote a hill, and is the origin of Croach and Craichmòre in Wigtownshire, and Crochmòre near Dumfries. It assimilates in form with *cnoc*, which, as has been pointed out, is always now pronounced *crochd*. Cròachy in Inverness-shire, and Crùchie in Aberdeenshire and Kirkcudbright, are from the adjectival form *cruachach*, full of stacks—*i.e.*, hilly—and the derivative *cruachán* gives rise to such names as Cròchan and Cràchan in Galloway; but Crèechan is most likely named from *criothachean* (creeghan), the aspens.

The names Aden in Aberdeenshire and Eden in many other counties are from *aodann*, the face or forehead, used to express the face or brow of a hill. There are streams of this name in Fife and Roxburgh, as well as the well-known river which flows past Carlisle. They have probably been named from the hill-brows overhanging them, just as the Gaelic *allt*, originally meaning a height (L. *altus*), came to mean a gorge between two heights, and ultimately the stream in the gorge.

Edendàrroch, in Dumbartonshire, is *aodann darach*, hill-brow of the oaks; Edinbèg, in Bute, the little brow; Edinbèlly, in Dumbartonshire, hill-brow of the *baile* or farm; Edinkìllie, in Moray, hill-brow of the wood.

Tulach, a hillock, a knoll, corresponds to the Broad Scots "knowe," but, although generally distributed over Ireland, it does not occur in Galloway or the Lowlands. Sir Walter Scott, by taking Craignethan Castle as his model of Tillietudlem, must be held responsible for the introduction of this prefix into Lanarkshire. It is owing to the renown of 'Old Mortality' that there is a station on the Caledonian Railway called Tillietudlem.

Tùlloch, Tùllich, Tùllo, Tòllo, and Tòlly are forms assumed by this word in names of places in the counties of Ross, Perth, Forfar, and Aberdeen; but when it occurs as a prefix, it generally assumes in the north-east the form of Tilly-, owing to the narrowing of the vowel-sounds peculiar to the peasantry of that district.

Sgorr or *sgurr*, a peak, is in all likelihood a loan from the Norse *sker*, a skerry, a sharp isolated rock in the sea, which gives also the Gaelic *sgeir* in the same sense, as well as the English "scaur" and "skerry." For this reason *sgorr* has no place in Irish topography, and in Scotland is found only in the counties of Inverness, Ross, and the north of Perthshire. There it is often found distinguishing peaked hills, as Sgurr na choinich (hōnigh), hill of the gathering (3260 feet); Sgurr a' bhealaich dheirg (a vallich harrig) (3376 feet), hill of the red pass; Sgurr a' choire ghlas (a horry hlass), hill of the green corrie, &c., all in Ross-shire.

Stob, though not found in Gaelic dictionaries, is of the same meaning as *sgurr*. There are Stob ban (3274 feet), the white "stob"; Stob choire an easain mhor (horrie an assan vore), "stob" of the corrie of the great waterfall (3658 feet), both in Inverness-shire; while in Wigtownshire we find the Stab Hill (725 feet).

Of similar meaning to *sgurr* and *stob* are *stac* and *stuc*, closely allied to English "stake," terms applied in the Highlands to conical hills, as Stac-meall-na-cuaich (3000 feet) in Inverness-shire—the hill-peak of the cuckoo; and Stuc-a-chroin (3184 feet), a conspicuous hill near Loch Earn. Stuckentàggart, near Drymen, is *stuc an t-shagairt*, the priest's peak; Stuckievièwlich, near Tarbet, on Loch Lomond—*stuc a' bhualaich* (vewaligh), peak of the cattle-fold; and there is a farm called Stuck in the Isle of Bute. Knockstòcks, a farm near Newton-Stewart, is appropriately named, for it is a hill studded with pointed knolls. This word has found its way into colloquial Scots in the term "stooks" for sheaves in a harvest-field.

Mam has the same meaning as *sliabh* and *monadh*, sometimes a moor, at others a mountain, but it is not of such common occurrence. Mamòre, in Perthshire, the great waste or mountain, has its converse in Mambèg, in Argyleshire, the little moor.

Their Lesson. 153

Leacán (lacken), a derivative of *leac*, a flagstone, is occasionally used to denote a sloping hillside, and may be recognised in Lèakin and Làkin in Wigtownshire, and Lauchentìlly near Kintore—*leacán tulaich*, slope of the hill. From another variant, *leacach* (lackagh), comes Lèckie, in Stirlingshire, most appropriately named from its position on the north flank of the Lennox range.

Airidh (airy), a shieling or hill-pasture, is better known among Galloway hills than elsewhere. In Man it is known as *cary* or *aeree*. It has no representation on the map of Ireland; but that it was once well established there appears from the 'Martyrology of Donegal,' in which at least half-a-dozen names are given beginning with that prefix. The annual summer migration of crofters driving their cattle to the *airidh* or hill-pastures was a leading feature in primitive pastoral life.

In Galloway this word has given names to such places as Airie, Airieòlland (twice)—*airidh olluin*, shieling of the wool; Airieglàssan—*airidh glasain*, shieling of the streamlet, &c. But Àiries in Wigtownshire, and Àros in Mull and again near Campbeltown, come from *aros*, a house.

Claen, sloping ground, gives its name to Clean near Perth, Clene in Kirkcudbright, Clyne in Aberdeen and Sutherland, &c.; the derivative *claenreach* forming Clènarie and Clèndrie near Inverary, and more than once in Wigtownshire, and Clènries near Dumfries. From another adjectival form come Clànnoch and Clènnoch in Kirkcudbright; Clànyard in Wigtownshire — *claen ard,* sloping height, the stress showing that *claen* is here the qualitative word; Clamdìsh in Kirkcudbright is *claen dess,* southern slope; and Clènter in Aberdeenshire, *claen tìr,* sloping land.

Carn, though specifically applied to an artificial heap, notably that over a grave, is often used to express a mountain. This may have arisen, in some instances, from the practice of burying distinguished personages on the tops of high hills, whence the hill would get the name of the grave on the top of it. Of the seven mountains in North Britain which rise above 4000 feet, two are distinguished with this prefix,—viz., Cairntòul—*carn tuathal,* north cairn; and Cairngòrm—*carn gorm,* blue cairn, both in Aberdeenshire. In Kirkcudbright there are, according to a local rhyme,—

"Cairnsmore of Fleet, and Cairnsmore of Dee,
And Cairnsmore of Carsphairn the biggest of the three."
(2600 feet.)

Carn is the same in all dialects of Celtic speech, and from the same root *car,* a rock, comes *creag* and *carraig* (Welsh *craig* and *careg*). Originally limited in meaning to a rock, or at most a cliff, *creag* has been extended in its application to denote high mountains, as Creag Mhor (vore) (3305 feet), great crag, and Creag Leacach in Inverness-shire (3238), crag of the flagstones or sloping crag, both in Perthshire.

The derivatives *creagach* and *creagán* give such names all over Scotland as Cràigie and Cràggan.

The earldom of Càrrick takes its name from some crag, but which particular one in that very craggy province there is now no means of knowing. Perhaps it was named from the big boulder on the march of Ayrshire and Galloway, known as the "Taxing Stone," from the duties which used to be levied there upon goods passing from one province to the other.

Iomaire (emery) is an obsolete word signifying a ridge or hill-back, surviving in the name Immervòulin, in Perthshire—*iomair mhuileain,* mill-ridge, a name which is familiar in the Anglo-Saxon form Milrig.

I have not recognised *fail* (foil), a cliff, which gives names to places in the south of Ireland, in our topography. In the north of Ireland it passes into *ail* (oil), and, though not now a living word in Scottish Gaelic, has at least been in use at some former time in Galloway, as is shown by the names of some hills in that district: Alhàng (21,200 feet), Alwhàt (1937 feet)—*ail chat* (haat), cliff of the wild cat; and Alwhìllan—*ail chuilean,* cliff of the whelps, or *chuilleain,* of the holly.

Cnap, a knob, perhaps has been borrowed from the Norse *knappr,* which has the same meaning. It expresses a knoll, but, as in *cnoc, n* following *k* has proved a stumbling-block to the Celts, and it is now pronounced "crap." There are places called Knap in Argyleshire and Perthshire, the Knaps in Aberdeenshire, and Kneep near Stornoway. The Nappers, on the flank of the Làmarken Hills near Newton-Stewart, is very like the Norse form; while from the adjectival form *cnapach*, a place of knolls, come Knàppoch in Aberdeenshire and Knìpoch near Oban. Knapèrna in Aberdeenshire seems to be *cnap fhearna* (erna), knoll of the alder; and Knàpdale has the Norse suffix, and, as Professor Mackinnon mentions, is called "The Crap" by the natives.

Torr, a round steep hill, generally of small elevation, is akin to the Latin *turris*. In fact, Irish *torr* and Welsh *twr* mean a tower, showing the same primitive suggestion that caused *dún*, primarily an enclosure or fort, to acquire the meaning of a hill, a down, because forts were ordinarily constructed on rising ground. The word enters into place-names all over the mainland of Scotland, even in the southeast, where there is Tòrwoodlee near Galashiels. This shows the old Gaelic embedded in an Anglian name. Tòrwood, near Larbert, was formerly Keltor —*coill torr*, wood hill; in the Selkirkshire example, A.S. *lea*, a field, has been superadded, so that Torwoodlee means "field of the hill wood."

The sandhills at the head of Luce Bay are called "The Torrs."

From the nominative plural *torran*, or the derivative *torrán*, come the names Tòrran in Caithness and Argyleshire, Tòrrance near Dumfries and Glasgow, and Tòrrans near Oban.

Ceide (keddy), "a compact kind of hill, smooth

and plain at the top" (O'Brien), generally appears in composition as Kitty: for example, Kittyshàlloch in Kirkcudbright is *ceide sealghe* (keddy shalluh), hill-brow of the hunting; and Kittiebrèwster in Aberdeenshire, Kittythrìstle in Selkirkshire, and Kittymùir in Lanarkshire, probably own a similar origin.

Dr Joyce mentions *cor* as an Irish word meaning a round hill, and although not now used in Scottish Gaelic, it may be recognised as the prefix of many names, though apt to be confused with *cathair* (caher), a fort, and *coire* (corry), a corrie. Core Hill is often met with between Aberdeen and the Mull of Galloway, but sometimes the reference seems to be to *cathair* (caher), a camp. Curleywèe, a summit of the Galloway hills, 2405 feet high, is probably *cor le gaeith* (gwee), hill in the wind; and Curnèlloch in the same range—*cor n'eilidh* (elly), hill of the hinds.

The derivative *corán* is more common: the Còran of Portmark is a hill in Kirkcudbright; Cornlèe is another—*corán liath* (lee), grey hill; and Còrran Lighthouse is in Loch Linnhe.

The commonest word expressing a stone is *clach*, Irish *cloch*, and it enters into a multitude of our place-names. Generally it is but little disguised as a prefix, but sometimes the aspirate disappears, as in Clayshànt,[1] formerly a parish in Wigtownshire, which Pont's spelling, Klacksant, shows to represent *clach seant*, the holy stone. At other times the older form *cloch* is preserved, as in Cloriddrick, a boulder on the

[1] The prefix cla- or clay- sometimes represents *cladh*, a mound.

north side of Lochwinnoch in Renfrewshire, supposed to perpetuate the name of Ryderch Hael, the celebrated ruler of Strathclyde in the sixth century.

The plural *clachan* is the recognised name for a hamlet, owing probably to the use of stones in forming foundations for the circular booths or wigwams in which the primitive inhabitants lived. It has been rendered familiar to Southerners in the immortal Clachan of Aberfoyle.

The derivative forms *clacheach, clacherin,* and *clachreach,* stony, a place of stones, produce a number of names: Clàchaig in Argyleshire and Clàchog in Arran, Clàchrum and Clàchrie in Wigtownshire, Clàuchrie near Girvan and again near Thornhill, Clàckrie near Auldgirth in Dumfriesshire.

A solitary stone on a sky-line, resembling a human figure, is sometimes called *buachaill,* a boy or herd, and thence becomes transferred to the hill itself. Dr Joyce notes this use of the word in Ireland, where it gives such hill-names as Bohilbreaga—*buachaill bregach,* mock or deceptive boy—to hills in Antrim, Down, and Limerick.

Some of the places called Bòwhill in Scotland may be a corruption of this word, and certainly Buachaill-Etive, a conspicuous summit in the Black Mount forest, is an instance of it, though strangers usually call it Bugle Ètive.

Bidean is a point or pinnacle, as Bidean-a'-ghlasthuill (3485 feet) in Ross-shire = point of the green hollow.

Dún is too well known among hill-names to be omitted from the list, though it is more commonly applied in its original and restricted sense of an enclosure or fortress, being closely related to A.S. *tún*, Eng. "town." Indeed it is so rare to find a hill that does not show traces of fortification that *dún* might apply equally to the hill and to what is on it. Probably Duncrùb in Dumbartonshire (3313 feet) may be correctly interpreted *dún craeb*, hill of the trees, like Moncreiff.

The diminutive or nominative plural *dúnan* yields innumerable names, like Dìnnans and Dìnnance in Ayrshire and Galloway, Dìnning and Dìnnings in Dumfriesshire, and Dòwnan near Ballantrae.

Bearna (barny) is a gap between two hills. Barnagèe in Wigtownshire is evidently the same as Barnageeha in Mayo, which is written in the 'Annals of the Four Masters' *Bearna gaoithe* (geuha, gwee), windy-gap. Barnbàuchle, also in Galloway, appears to be the same as *bearna bocghail* of the Irish Annalists, meaning the gap of danger. In Wigtownshire also occurs Craigbèrnoch—*creag bearnach*; and not far distant is found the exact translation in Cloven Craig. In the same county Glenvèrnoch shows the sound of the aspirated *b*, though Pont writes it in the original form—Glenbarranach.

Another, and commoner, word for a pass between hills is *bealach* (ballagh), appearing in Welsh as *bwlch*. It has received the secondary meanings of a

Passes.

crossing-place, ford, or road; hence in Manx *boallagh* is the usual word for a road. The ancient battle-cry of the 88th Regiment, or Connaught Rangers, is "Fág a' bealach!"—"Clear the road!" In many counties there are places simply named Bàlloch, which in Fife and Perth is softened into Bàllo. Ballochalèe and Ballochabèastie in Wigtownshire are *bealach na' laogh* (leuh) and *bealach na' biasta* (beastie), the passes of the calves and of the cattle. The latter is the name of a gateway on Culròy farm.

Hollows. The converse of a hill is *lag* or *lagán*, a hollow or low place, and, nearly as this resembles E. "low," especially in the Broad Scots "laigh," the meaning of the Gaelic has been completely forgotten in the Lowlands, and it is a common thing to find elevations called Lag Hill and Làggan Hill, from the hollows at their feet.

The vowel-sound is variable, and the word forms prefixes in Lig, Lug, Liggan, Luggan, and Logan. Lògan is the name of places in Galloway, Dumfries, Ayrshire, Lanark, and Mid-Lothian, while Lògie occurs in Perthshire and the north-eastern counties.

Glac is the old word for the palm of the hand, and is figuratively given as the name of depressions in the land, causing such names as Glack in Perthshire and Aberdeenshire, and Glaik in Bute and Wigtownshire.

Cabhan (cavan, cowan), a hollow, probably ought to be written *camhan*, as being from the prolific root *cam*, curved, bent. In Welsh it takes the form *cwm*, a combe or dingle.[1] There are several places in Dumfriesshire and Galloway called Còwan, Càven, and Càvens.

Cúl, the back, and *cuil*, a corner or nook, assume the same forms, Cool-, Cul-, and Kil-, in composition, and are liable to confusion not only with each other but also with *coill*, a wood, and *cil*, the locative case of *ceall*, a cell or chapel. There are several places called Cuil in Galloway and Argyleshire, which evidently mean a corner; but Cuildrỳnach on Loch Fyne may be either the corner, the hill-back, or the wood of the thorns (*draighneach*).

Culràin in Ross-shire is the same word as Coleraine in Ireland, which is explained in the Tripartite Life of St Patrick to mean *cuil rathain*, corner of the ferns, translated by Colgan *secessus filicis*.

Culscàdden is a farm named from a creek on Wigtown Bay—*cuil scadan*, corner of the herrings—*i.e.*, a place where herrings were landed—and has its exact parallel in Culscùdden in Dublin county; but Culmòre in Wigtownshire is *coill mór*, great wood, as the large roots still embedded in the soil of that farm testify, a name which in another part of the same county has become Killiemòre, just as in Cork county it appears as Kilmore (written by the Annalists *coill mohr*), and in Connemara Kylemore and Cuilmore.

[1] The original stem is *ku*, to contain, whence Latin *cavea*, Eng. *cave*.

Gleann (glen), a glen, Welsh *glyn*, has been so completely adopted into English speech that it is not necessary to dwell on its importance as a component of place-names.

Coire (curry) also, in its application to an elevated basin or "corrie" in the hill, is almost equally well understood. The literal meaning of the word is a caldron, and its figurative use to describe surface contour is precisely similar in idea to that of the Greek κρατήρ, a cup, which we continue to apply to the crater of a volcano. But besides its hollow form, a caldron is associated with seething, and *coire* is used to express a troubled pool in a river. Thus Corra Linn, one of the Falls of Clyde, is the caldron pool. But Corra Pool on the Dee, near Kirkcudbright, must be explained as from *coradh*, a fish-weir. Corvìsel (pron. Corveazle), near Newton-Stewart, is written by Pont Kerivishel, and probably means *coire iseal* (eeshal), the low pool, being situated on the bank of the first pool above the tide, or the lowest in the river Cree.

Bun, the bottom or lower end, enters into many names, such as Bonèssan near Oban—*bun easain*, foot of the waterfall; and Bunàwe, the foot of Loch Awe. Bonèen, at Lamlash, is the diminutive *bunín*.

Ton, the rump, is used topographically in a peculiar way. It sometimes means low-lying bottom-land, but in the curious name Tandragèe or Tonderghìe, occurring in Galloway and Arran, as well as very frequently in Ireland under these forms or as

Tonlegee and Tonregee, the meaning is *ton le gaeith* (geuh, gwee), backside to the wind, graphically descriptive of a place where cattle stand in storm with their tails to the wind.

Earball, the tail, used in modern Gaelic in a contemptuous sense, was applied to express the end of a ridge or a long strip of land. There are places in Ross-shire called Arboll and Arble, corresponding to Urbal, Erribul, and Rubble in Ireland. In Wigtownshire, Darnàrbel—*dobhar* (dour) *an earbuill*—seems to mean the water of the tail, as the Grey Mare's Tail is often given as a name for a waterfall.

Currach, a marsh, not known in modern Gaelic, Marshes. gives names to many places in Ireland, but runs into the same forms as *coire*, a caldron. Cùrrie in Mid-Lothian and Cùrrah near Girvan are probably derived from this word.

A commoner term for bog-land is *riasg*, to which, with its derivative *riasgach*, boggy, may be traced Risk in Renfrewshire, Rìskend near Kilsyth, Rìskhouse in Aberdeenshire, Rùskich near Aberfeldy, Rùskie near Stirling, and Rùsco in Kirkcudbright, corresponding to many places called Risk, Riesk, and Roosky in Ireland.

Caedh (kay), a bog, or, as it is called in Lowland Scots, "quaw," suggests a connection with the English "quagmire," but it is not clearly made out, for the latter word is in reality "quakemire." Culkàe, a farm in Wigtownshire, is *cùl caedha*, back or corner of the bog.

Crithlach (creelagh), a shaking bog, from *crith*, to tremble, gives Cràilloch, the name of two farms in Wigtownshire and another near Girvan, and Crỳla in Aberdeenshire.

Tol, a hole or hollow, remains in names like Toldòw, in Aberdeenshire—*tol dubh*, black hole; Tolrònald near Oban—*tol Raonuill*, Ronald's hole; and Bidean a' ghlas thuill, a hill in Ross-shire (3485 feet), means peak of the green hollow.

Lod or *lodán* is a wet place, a swamp or pool: hence Cumlòden in Kirkcudbright and Cumlòdden in Argyleshire—*cam lodain*, the bend of the swamp; and Cullòden—*cúl lodain*, back of the swamp. Lodnigàpple—*lod nan capul*, swamp of the horses; Loddanmòre—*lodán mór*, great swamp; Loddanrèe—*lodán fhraeich* (hree), heather-bog, are other examples; and "The Lòdens" is the name given to swampy pools in Polbae Burn, all in Wigtownshire.

Meadows. Now I will pass over a number of names descriptive of natural land-surface, such as *cluan*, a meadow, giving Clune in Banff and Clone in Galloway, Clonfin near Kilmarnock—*cluan fionn*, the white meadow, and Clonskèa near Blairgowrie—*cluan sgitheach*, hawthorn-meadow; with its plural, *cluainte*, giving Clòintie near Maybole and Clantibùies in Wigtownshire—*cluainte buidhe*, yellow meadows; *leana* (lenna), also meaning a meadow, giving Lènnie Mains near Cramond, Lèny near Callander, Lenziebèg near Garnkirk, and Lenagbòyach near Greenock—*leana bathaich* (baach), meadow of the cow-house; *tamhnach* (tawnah), an obsolete name for meadow, which remains in Tànnoch near Glasgow and in Kirkcudbright, Tànnach near Wick, Tànnock in Ayrshire and Kirkcudbright, and Tannyflùx—*tamhnach fliuch*, wet meadow, Tannyròach—*tamhnach ruadh*, red meadow, in Wigtownshire; *reidh* (ray), flat land, yielding Reay in Sutherlandshire, Rephàd near Stranraer—*reidh fada*, long flat, Rebèg near Beauly, Raemòre in Kincardine, and Remòre in Fife; *scrath*, sward, producing Scraphàrd near Fochabers, *scrath ard*, corrupted strangely into Scrapehàrd in Aberdeenshire.

All these I just mention and pass on, leaving many more unmentioned, in order to notice names which have more to do with human occupation.

Dabhach (davach), a measure of land, is originally, as Professor Mackinnon has shown, a measure of capacity, and was applied to denote the extent of land which required a *davoch* of corn to sow it. In Ireland *dabhach* means a vat, and is applied figuratively, as Scottish Highlanders do *coire* (corry, kirry), a kettle, to describe deep hollows in the land. It has been supposed to have been the regular unit of land-measure among the Picts, but there is no trace of it among the place-names of Galloway. In Dàvo in Kincardineshire the word remains alone. Davochbèg and Davochfìn in Sutherland are *dabhach beag* and *dabhach fionn*, the little and the white davach; Dochfòur and Dochgàrroch in Inverness-shire—*dabhach fuar*, the cold davach, and *dabhach garbh* (garriv), rough davach.

<small>Land measures.</small>

The Broad Scots "doach," a fish-weir or cruive, is probably the same word, from the receptacle in which salmon were taken; and Culdòch on the Dee, near Kirkcudbright, means "back of the fish-weir," *cúl dabhaich*.

Roinn, older *rinn*, *rind*, a point of land, is commonly used to denote a division of ground. The term "run-rig," applied to a primitive mode of agrarian tenure still surviving in the Western Highlands and Islands, is a corruption of *roinn-ruith* (rinn ruee), or division-running. *Ruith*, a running or course, has taken the form of the English "rig"; and by a strange perversity *roinn*, which means a rig, has become "run." Airdrie, in Lanark, Fife, Moray, and Kirkcudbright, is *ard ruith*, high pasture-run. Ringuinea in Wigtownshire is *roinn Cinaeidh*, Kenneth's portion; but Ringdòo in Luce Bay is *roinn dubh*, black point, and Ringielàwn at the head of Loch Trool is *roinn na' leamhan*, point of the elms. This is also called the Soldiers' Holm, for here it is said that Lord Essex's men, slaughtered in combat with Robert the Bruce, were buried.

Pennylands.

Professor Mackinnon has shown how the Norse *unga* or ounce, composed of eighteen or twenty pennies, was adopted in Gaelic land-tenure in the west; and he quotes Pennyghàel, the Gael's pennyland; Pennygòwn, the smith's penny-land; Penmòlach—*peighinn molach*, rough or grassy penny-land, as instances in the place-names of Mull. It is easy to see how the Gaelic *peighinn*, a penny, in Manx *ping*, complicates the use of *pen* as a test for Welsh place-names.

Leffindònald near Ballantrae—*leth pheighin Don-uil*, Donald's halfpenny-land; and Lefnòl on Loch Ryan, written Leffynollock in 1456 and Lefnollo two years later, is, strange as it may seem, all that remains of *leth pheighin Amhalghaidh*, Olaf's or Aulay's halfpenny-land. After all, the spelling *leth pheighinn* (ley fein) for the sound of "leffin" is not more out of the way than halfpenny for Scottish "ha'p'ny."

Garwòling in Argyleshire used to be written Garforling—*garadh feorlin*, farthing-land; and *clitag*, the eighth part of a penny, seems to account for Clùtag, a farm in Wigtownshire.

The whole system of ancient land-measurement, far too intricate to enter upon in a discussion of place-names, has been ably treated by the late Mr Skene, who traced the overlapping of the Saxon and Scandinavian systems. The sentence with which he concluded his examination of the question gives the position as he left it, and it is scarcely possible to carry it further:—

The two systems of land measurement appear to meet in Galloway, as in Carrick we find measure by penny-lands, which gradually become less frequent as we advance eastward, where we encounter the extent by merks and pounds, with an occasional appearance of a pennyland, and of the bovate or oxgang in church-lands.

But there is one word I must allude to, because

it is so common and often so deeply disguised—
that is *ceathramh* (carrow), or, as Irish writers love
to express the same sound, *ceathramhadh*, a fourth
part or quarter. In English-speaking districts of
Scotland it has been worn down to the prefix car,
cur, kir, kirrie, and recourse must be had to early
spellings to distinguish it from *cathair*, a fort; *carr*,
a rock; or *coire*, a corrie.

Carmìnnow in Kirkcudbright was written Kirre-
monnow as late as 1615 — *ceathramh monaidh*
(carrow munney), moorland quarter; Kirmìnnoch
in Wigtownshire, between the abbeys of Glenluce
and Saulseat, appears in 1505 as Kerowmanach—
ceathramh manach, monk's quarter-land; Leùcarrow
in Wigtownshire is *leth ceathramh*, half-quarter land,
like Leakarroo, a farm in the Isle of Man.

Occupations and trades.
In the primitive Celtic community there were in
each *clachan* or village two persons of whom it would
be hard to say which was the more important. One
was *bard*, the rhymer, whose title in the singular
number appears in names like Drumavàird in South
Ayrshire—*druim a' bhaird* (vaird), and Knockenbàird in Aberdeenshire, *cnoc an baird*; and in the
plural, Barnbòard in Kirkcudbright, written in 1599
Barnebard—*barr na' bard*, hill-top of the poets.

The other was *gobha* (gow), the smith, whose name
in the genitive, *gobhan*, has been preserved in almost
every parish. The only word with which it is likely
to be confused is *gamhan* (gowan), a calf, which
probably gives Blairgòwan near Stirling, and Blairin-

gòne near Dollar, the calves' field. Both *gobha* and *gamhan* have become personal names, Gow and Gavin. Shades of meaning are often accurately preserved in spite of the wear and tear of ages, for Auchengòwnie, near Bridge of Earn, is formed from another word, *gamhnach* (gownah), a milch-cow.

Tealach, the smith's forge, yields the name Challoch, so common in Galloway; *ceard*, a tinker, gives Glencàird in Kirkcudbright; *saor*, a carpenter, is difficult to recognise, because when the *s* is aspirated into silence in the genitive, it is customary to replace it by *t*, a process which Irish grammarians distinguish as eclipse. Thus Macintyre is *mac an t-shaoir*, the carpenter's son. Balshère, Balsìer, and Baltìer, in Wigtownshire, may be either the carpenter's house, or *baile siar* or *tiar*, the west house. But Drummatìer, in the same county, is probably *druim a' t-shaoir*, the carpenter's ridge.

The old name for a tanner, *sudaire*, is subject to the same process: hence Bentùdor and Lagtùtor in Wigtownshire are *beinn t-shudaire* (tudory) and *lag t-shudaire* (tudory), the tanner's hill and hollow.

Greusach originally meant an embroiderer, but came to mean a shoemaker, and Balgràcie in Wigtownshire (Pont, Balgresy) is *baile greusaich*, the shoemaker's house. With masons we approach medieval times; but Stronachlàcher on Loch Katrine is a name of respectable antiquity, *sron a' chlachair*, the mason's point; and we find Beinn a' chlachair in Ardverikie Forest. *Buachail,* a shepherd, is transmogrified into Knockbògle in Galloway; and Bugle Ètive, a hill in the Black Mount Forest, is the same word, not seldom applied metaphorically to a peaked hill. The hangman, *crochadhair,* had a busy time in old days, and Auchenròcher near Stranraer and Knockròger in Kirkcudbright — *achadh* and *cnoc chrochadhair* (hroghair) — commemorate his office; while Knockcrosh, Auchencròsh, and Barncròsh are the gallows-hill, from *crois,* the gallows. It is not a long step thence to *mearlach,* a thief, a word preserved in Knockamàirly and Knockmàrloch, two places in Wigtownshire.

Nor is there wanting record of the misfortunes of humanity. Bellybòcht Hill, near Thornhill, is the same as Ballybòught, a suburb of Dublin—*baile bochd,* poor man's house.

From *lobhar* (lure), a leper or scrofulous person, many names are derived, such as Drumlòur near Thornhill, Barlùre and Ochtralùre in Wigtownshire, the leper's hill and upland, Craiglùre in Ayrshire, leper's crag, &c. Liberton, the Anglo-Saxon equivalent to leper's house, occurs in Mid-Lothian and Lanarkshire. The Mid-Lothian Liberton was so named as far back as the reign of Malcolm Canmore, for it is mentioned as having been resorted to by sick persons on account of St Catherine's "Oyliewell" or Balm Well. On a wild piece of moorland on the border of Wigtownshire and Ayrshire is a place called Lìberland, leper's land; and close by is Carlùre, *ceathramh lobhar* (carrow lure), the leper's quarter-land.

I pass over names of rivers and lakes rapidly but reluctantly, for river-names are among the oldest we have. Running water is very often described from its roughness *garbh*, and this gives a host of names whence the generic *amhuinn* has dropped— as Gàrry in Perth and Inverness, Gryfe in Renfrew, and Yàrrow in Selkirk, already alluded to. Gàrrel, a parish in Dumfriesshire, formerly Gàrvald, Gàrvald in East Lothian, Gàrrel in Argyle, Gàrrald in Dumbartonshire, Gàrvel in Stirlingshire, are all *garbh allt*, rough stream; Gàrpol in Dumfries is *garbh pol*, rough water; Gàrland in Kirkcudbright —*garbh linn*, rough pool.

The windings of a stream earned it the epithet *cam*, twisted—as Càmelon, a parish in Stirlingshire —*cam linn*, curved pool, the same as Lincòm, a salmon-pool on the Luce in Wigtownshire. Càmisk in Ayrshire and Càmiskie on the Lochy are *cam uisce*, winding water. Càmple Burn in Dumfriesshire is *cam pol*, with the same meaning.

Fìnglas in Perthshire, and Fìnlas, a stream in Dumbarton, stand for *fionn glas*, white water, just as Dòuglas, in many places, is *dubh glas*, black water. Dìpple or Dìppol is a common stream-name—that is, *dubh pol*, black water; the Duisk in Ayrshire is *dubh uisce;* and the Doon in that county is not named, as has been supposed, from Doon Castle in Loch Doon, but the castle takes its name from the river—*dubh*

Rivers and streams.

amhuinn, black water. Where the river Doon leaves its parent loch it pours a cataract through a wooded glen, now called the Ness Glen, from *an eas*, the cascade. Another form of *dubh amhuinn* is Dèvon, a tributary to the Forth, and a river of that name in Fife is actually known as the Black Devon, so completely has the meaning of the old title been lost.

Ecclesiastical names.   All ecclesiastical names must, of course, have been introduced subsequently to the fourth century, when Christianity can first be certainly affirmed to have been preached in Scotland.

It is true that missionaries had been at work within the Roman province of Valentia before the advent of Ninian in 397, but he is the earliest evangelist of whom we have definite information. His name occurs very frequently on our maps, but often, by the common tendency to change *n* to *r*, it becomes Ringan; for, strangely enough, Kilnìnian in Mull, near Tobermòry (*tiobar Muire*, Mary's Well), is probably a dedication to St Nennidius, a friend of St Bride's, in the fifth century. Killantrìngan in Wigtownshire and South Ayrshire are *cill shaint* (keel ant) *Ringain;* Chipperdìngan in Wigtownshire is *tiobar Dingain*, another form of his name, as in Geoffery Gaimars's 'Estorie des Engles' (twelfth century):—

"A Witernen gist Saint Dinan
Long tens vint devant Columban."

It is strange to find his name adopted by the Norsemen after the lapse of at least four centuries.

North Ronaldshay, which Ninian is supposed to have visited, is Rinansey, Rinan's Isle. It is still stranger to find that his name is not attached to Whithorn, where he began his great work. He dedicated his church there to St Martin; but three miles distant, on the coast of Glasserton, is a cave long known as St Ninian's Cave, which yielded to exploration some ten years ago abundant confirmation of the tradition. Under many tons of *débris* were found the remains of a chapel and no fewer than eighteen crosses, either carved in the living rock or hewn out of separate stones. Here is a notable instance of the adhesion of a place-name, for it must be remembered that Galloway lapsed into paganism after the death of Ninian.

It must not be supposed that all the land-names formed of the personal names of Ninian and other saints are as old as the era of the persons they commemorate. Many of them are subsequent dedications, in accordance with the practice continued to this day.

The long list of Scottish saints would soon become wearisome: it is only necessary to mention some of those names which are most obscure. When the name is Celtic, the saint's name forms the suffix, as Kilmòry in Argyleshire, Renfrewshire, Bute, and Arran—*cill Muire;* when it is Saxon it forms the prefix, as Màrykirk, a parish in Kincardine. But the Gael borrowed the A.S. *circ* or the Norse *kirkja*, and so we get Kirkchrìst in Kirk-

Churches.

cudbright, *circ Crioisd,* Christ Church, Kirkbrìde in many places, Kirkcòlm in Wigtownshire, as well as Kilchrìst near Campbelton, Kirkmìchael and Kilmìchael, Kilbrìde in twenty-one places in Scotland, and Kilmalcòlm in Renfrewshire. Kirkdòminie near Colmonell is *circ Domini,* Church of the Lord; and Kirkpà'dy Fair is still held in the Mearns, commemorating St Palladius. I will ask you to pause for a moment on Kilmalcòlm, for railway influence, I am sorry to say, is prevailing to corrupt it into Kilmàlcolm. The second *l* is no part of the name; in the twelfth century it was rightly written Kilmakolme. *Ma* or *mo* is an endearing prefix to a saint's name, very commonly used, and may be recognised in Kirkmabreck—*circ ma Brice* (breekie), the church of our Brecan, or St Bricius, of whom many interesting, but scarcely edifying, stories are told in the Breviary of Aberdeen.

This prefix *ma* or *mo* is often confused with the prefix *mael,* the shaven one, and Màlcolm, the personal name, is *mael Coluim,* Columba's servant.

Kilmaròn in Fife and Kilmarònock in Dumbarton are named from St Ronan—Ronog being an alternative form of Ronan; and Rònay off Raasay, and Ròna sixty miles north-east of Lewes, are both N. *Rögn ey,* Ronan's isle; but Kilmàrnock, which might be supposed identical with Kilmarònock, is *cill ma Ernainuig,* church of our Ernanog (diminutive of Ernan), uncle of St Columba.

Hillmabrèedia in Wigtownshire is an unusual

form, *chill ma Brighde,* cell of our Bridget: it is situated on the Breedie Burn, St Bride's stream.

There seems to be no Celtic dedication in Scotland to St John except Kildàlton in Islay, *cill daltain,* the church of the foster-brother, and Killèan in Cantyre, which is a contracted form of *cill Sheathainn* (hane), a form of *Ian* or *Eoin,* English *John.*

St Kentigern, evangelist of Strathclyde in the seventh century, has left his familiar name, Mungo (the gracious), impressed firmly on the scene of his labours, awkwardly metamorphosed in Strathbùngo —*srath Mungo.* His mother, St Thennat or Thenew, was commemorated in a church in Glasgow known at the Reformation as San Theneuke's Kirk—now St Enoch's.

The Celtic *eaglais,* a church, has been sorely mutilated in Lesmahàgow—*eaglais Machuti,* but remains unimpaired in Ecclefèchan—*eaglais Fechain* or *fitheachain* (little raven).

I have alluded in a former lecture to some of the forms taken by the prefix *lann,* W. *llan,* a church; I need therefore do no more than mention one or two more. Lamlàsh in Arran is *lann mo Lais,* church of St Molio or Molassi. The cave there is known as St Molio's cave. Lumphànan, a parish in Aberdeenshire where Macbeth is said to have been killed, and Lumphìnnans in Fife, are probably churches of St Finan, who was called Winnin in Welsh, and has been commemorated in that form at Kilwìnning in Ayrshire and Kirkgùnzeon (pronounced Kirkgunnion), written in the twelfth century Kirkwynnin, in Kirkcudbright. Close to Kirkmàiden in the Machars of Wigtownshire is a field called Long Maidens—that is, *lann Medainn,* St Medana's church. Langbèdholm, near Moffat, is *lann Bedleim,* church of Bethlehem.

Wells. Wells of old were dedicated and blessed as regularly as churches; hence we often find *tiobar,* a well, prefixed to the names of saints. In the south-west this word becomes Chipper, often changed into Chapel. Instances of this are—Chipperfinian in Wigtownshire, St Finan's well; Chipperdàndy near Glenluce—*tiobar shaint Antoin,* St Anthony's well; and in the same parish is a stream called Piltànton—*pol shaint Antoin* (*sh* silent); Chipperhèron or Chapelhèron near Whithorn—*tiobar Chiarain,* St Kieran's well. Sometimes it becomes Kibbert, as in Kibberty Kìte Well near the Mull of Galloway, which, seeing that it is on a piece of land called Katrine's Croft, it is not difficult to recognise as *tiobar tigh Cait,* the well of Catherine's house. Tibbers, near Drumlanrig, is locally supposed to have been named after the Emperor Tiberius! but it requires but a slight acquaintance with the place to recognise *tiobar* in this form, for there is a celebrated well of great size within the ruined tower.

Monasteries and clergy. The old name for a monastery was *manaisdir,* which remains in Knockmànister in South Ayrshire, and Auchenmànister, close to Glenluce Abbey; and *manach,* a monk, sometimes assuming the same form

Their Lesson.

as *meadhonach* (mennoch), middle, occurs very frequently. Thus Auchmànnoch near Kilmarnock is the same as Mònkscroft near Auchteràrder, but Ballymènach and Balmìnnoch in many places is the same as Midton or Middleton.

A friar was *brathair* (brair), whence Altibràir and Portbrìar in Wigtownshire, the friar's glen and port.

Sagart, a priest, is generally altered in the genitive singular to *haggard* by aspiration, or *taggart* by eclipse, as Bartàggart in Wigtownshire; but it remains unchanged as the genitive plural in Balsàggart near Maybole. Balnàb near Whithorn Priory, and again near Glenluce Abbey, is *baile an aib*, the abbot's land; and of course the surname MacNab is *mac an aib*, abbot's son, just as Mac-Taggart is *mac an t-shagairt*, priest's son. *Honi soit qui mal y pense:* the rule of celibacy was not strictly enforced upon the clergy of the primitive Church. M'Chlery, again, is *mac clereich*, the clerk's or clergyman's son, a word which yields the place-names Barneycleàry, *barr na' clerech*, hill of the clergy, Clàry, and Portacleàrys in Wigtownshire, Leffinclèary in South Ayrshire—*leth pheighinn* (ley flinn) *clereich*, parson's halfpenny-land, and Auchenclèary, the parson's field.

I have already explained the derivation of Gillèspie in Wigtownshire from *cill espuig*, the bishop's cell: I have little doubt that in the other extremity of Scotland, Gòlspie, or as it is locally pronounced Gheispie, in Sutherland, is the same name, for in

1330 it is written Goldespy and in 1550 Golspie-kirktoun.

The Gael intended no disrespect when he called a recluse or holy person *naomh* (nave). Oilean-na-Naomh in the Western Isles is the Isle of Saints, and Kilnàve near Greenock, the saint's cell.

<small>Land not usually named by early Celts from ownership.</small> The Psalmist has said that the inward thought of men is "that their houses shall continue for ever, and their dwelling-places to all generations: they call their lands after their own names." This was perhaps less the case with the Celts than with other races, owing to the peculiarity of their land tenure. Land was possessed by the tribe, not by the individual; such cultivation as was carried on was worked on the wasteful run-rig system, and pasture was held in common. The land, therefore, of the tribe or sept was often called after the chief himself, as Lorn, after Loarn, first king of the Scots in Dalriada, or Kyle, after Coel Hen—old King Cole; or after the tribe, as Slamannan, the moor of the Picts of Manann. But when the subdivisions of land bear the name of an individual, it is more likely, if the name be an ancient one, that it commemorates some act or incident than that it indicates possession.

For instance, there were two kings Alpin: the first, Alpin, son of Eochadh, king of a section of Picts, who invaded the Picts of Galloway, and after conquering that province was slain by a man hid in a wood as he rode across a ford in the year 741. The stream is now the App, the glen Glenàpp, a contraction of Alpin; and the farm on the south of the glen is named after a large stone upon it, Laichtàlpin—*lecht Alpin,* Alpin's grave. The other Alpin, king of the Scots, had some bloody encounters with the Picts in 834, and Pitèlpie near Dundee—*pett Alpin,* Alpin's farm, not because he owned it, but because he died there, is traditionally pointed out as the place where he was killed and beheaded by them. Rathèlpie near St Andrews is supposed to have been his centre of operations—*rath Alpin,* Alpin's fort.

The establishment of the feudal system in the Lowlands brought individuals into closer connection with the land as proprietors and tenants, and then, doubtless, such ground as had not yet been named would often receive the name of the cultivator. On the whole, however, you will find that Celtic land-names, as a rule, are formed to denote some peculiarity of surface, position, product, or some incident occurring or occupation carried on there.

It is otherwise with Teutonic names. Personal names are exceedingly frequent in their formation. A large proportion of names ending in A.S. *ton* or *ham,* and in the Norse *by* or *bólstaðr,* indicating settled dwelling, have a personal name as a prefix. Surnames may be said to have been unknown until the thirteenth century. A very good instance of their origin is given by Camden, who says :—

In late times, in the time of Henry VIII., an ancient worshipful gentleman of Wales, being called at the pannel

of a jurie by the name of Thomas Ap William Ap Thomas
Ap Richard Ap Hoel Ap Evan Vaghan, &c., was advised
by the judge to leave that old manner; whereupon he
afterwards called himself Moston, according to the name
of his principal house, and left that surname to his
posterity.

<small>Land-owners named from their lands.</small>
Men in possession or occupation of lands generally
took their surname in this way, and then arose a
curious process when such names were conferred
afresh upon other lands. I cannot give you a better
instance of this than is afforded by my own surname—a tolerably common one in Scotland. In the
eleventh century, Maccus the son of Unwin became
possessed of certain lands on the Tweed. Here there
was an excellent salmon-pool, just below Kelso
bridge, which became known as *Maccus' wiel*, the
A.S. for a pool, now Màxwheel. This name got
attached to the surrounding lands, hence members
of the family became known as Aymer, John, or
Herbert de Maccuswell, for apparently they thought
more highly of their salmon-pool than of the house
near St Boswells, Màxton—*Maccus tún*. As time
went on, the preposition was dropped and the family
became simple Maxwells. But they prospered and
obtained other lands, and so we find the name,
which was originally a place-name, having become
a surname, becoming a place-name once more, as
Maxwellton, Maxwellfield, and Maxwellheugh.

And now, ladies and gentlemen, having led you

thus far, you may turn to me and say, What does it all mean? to what conclusion have you brought us? Well, so far as any new light upon history or any novel theory or confirmation of former theory is concerned, the conclusion is a lame and impotent one. We may listen in land-names to the voices of successive races that have peopled our country; we may understand from them much concerning the landscape of a bygone age and the creatures that lived in it; we may obtain from them evidence confirming what we have learnt from history; they may even, in a few instances, help to set right mistaken readings of history, as in the notable example of the Arthurian topography so luminously and cautiously elaborated by the late Mr Skene. But beyond that they are *vox et præterea nihil*.

Conclusion.

But one lesson we have learnt, that much confusion is thrown into history by clumsy or corrupt spellings of place-names, and in the present advanced state of science it will be discreditable to this generation if it passes away without something having been done to prevent further corruption of names. And in attempting to do this, let me add a few words as to the right method of investigation. I am only repeating what I have already said; but this is a matter indispensable to progress in this branch of archæology—a branch, I believe, far behind any other in scientific method.

Let students avoid construing names merely on the ground of similarity of syllables to words.

Letters are very deceptive things, and guessing etymology is of all pursuits the most deceptive. If there could be found some one in every county of Scotland to prepare lists of all the land-names therein, giving the earliest spellings, and the exact local pronunciation, and *carefully marking the stressed syllables*, we should soon arrive at a degree of knowledge in the matter which it is beyond the power of any single man to accomplish. This has been done already for some of the islands by the late Captain Thomas, a valued Fellow of this Society. His MS. lists are in our possession, and form a perfect model of the way that kind of thing should be done.

I will only say, in conclusion, that I am gratified by the degree of attention which this subject has already received; and I beg to thank you warmly for the patience with which you have followed me in an intricate and perhaps tedious inquiry.

INDEX OF PLACE-NAMES REFERRED TO IN THE TEXT.

ABBREVIATIONS.

G., Gaelic.
O.G., Old Gaelic.
W., Welsh.   P., Pictish.
N., Old Norse or Danish.

A.S., Anglo-Saxon.
M.E., Middle English.
O.N.E., Old Northern English.
L., Latin.

The stress syllable in each name is indicated by the accent, as Kilmòry.

	PAGE
Achnabà—G. *achadh na ba*, the cow's field	125
Achnacàrry—G. *achadh na coraidh* (corry), field of the fish-weir	133
Achnacòne—G. *achadh na' con*, field of dogs	127
Aden—G. *aodann*, the forehead, brow of a hill	150
Æ (river)—N. *á*, a river	86
Afflèck—G. *achadh na leac* (leck), field of the flagstones	133
Aìket } A.S. *ác wudu*, oak wood Aìtket }	107
Air—N. *eyrr*, the beach	87
Aìrdrie—G. *ard ruith* (rew), high pasture-run	166
Airds—G. *ard*, the height	147
Àirie—G. *airidh* (airy), a shieling, or mountain pasture	153
Airieglàssan—G. *airidh glasain*, shieling of the streamlet	153
Airieòlland—G. *airidh* (airy) *olluin*, shieling of the wool	153

Airiequhìllart—G. *airidh ubhal ghart* (owlhart), apple-
    yard shieling 137
Àiries—G. *aros*, a house 153
Aith—G. *ait*, a house-site 78
Aldòuran—G. *allt doran*, otter-stream . . . 128
Àllarshaw—A.S. *alr scaga*, alder-wood . . . 112
Allerbeck—A.S. *alr becc*, N. *ölr bekk*, alder-stream . 10
Almond (rivers)—O.G. *amuin*, a river . . . 7, 8
Altàggart Burn—G. *allt shagairt* (taggart), priest's glen
    or burn 18
Altibràir—G. *allt a' brathair* (brair), friar's stream . 177
Alwhàt—G. *ail chat* (hwat), cliff of the wild cat . . 155
Alwhìllan—G. *ail chuilean* (hwillan), cliff of the whelps,
    or *chuilleain* (hwillan), of the holly . . . 155
Appleby—N. *epla by*, apple-house 137
Applecròss—G. *aber Crossain*, mouth of the Crossan . 137
Àpplegarth—N. *epla garðr*, apple-yard . . . 137
Arble ⎱ G. *earball*, the tail, the end of a ridge, or a strip
Àrboll ⎰   of land 163
Ardàchy—G. *ard achaidh*, hill of the cultivated field . 134
Ardentìnny—G. *ard an teine* (tinny), beacon height . 147
Ardentrìve—G. *ard an t-shnaoimh* (trave), headland of
    the swimming 42
Ardgòur—G. *ard gobhar* (gowr), goat's height . . 22
Ardmòre—G. *ard mór*, great height 15
Àrdoch—G. *ard achadh* or *mhagh* (vah), high field . 134
Ardrìshaig — G. *ard driseag* (drissagh), thorny height
                                                    114, 147
Ardròssan—G. *ard rosain*, height of the little headland . 147
Argỳle—G. *earra Gaidheal* (gael), the Gael's boundary . 98
Àrnfìnlay—G. *earran*, Finlay's land 136
Àros—G. *aros*, a house 153
Àscock ⎱ N. *askr vik*, ship's creek 90
Àscog ⎰

Index of Place-Names.

Athole—? P. *ath Fotla*, Fotla's ford . . . 36, 58
Attachòirrin—G. *atta chaoruinn* (hearrun), rowan-tree house 112
Auchabrìck—G. *achadh bruic*, badger's field . . 129
Auchencleàry—G. *achadh an clereich*, parson's field . 177
Auchèncrosh—G. *achadh an crois*, gallows field . . 170
Auchencròw ⎱ G. *achadh na craebh* (aha na creuve),
Auchencrùive ⎰ field of trees 107
Auchendràin—G. *achadh na' draighean* (drane), field of blackthorns 114
Auchengìlshie—G. *achadh giolchach*, broom field . . 117
Auchengòwnie — G. *achadh na gamhnaich* (gownah), milch-cow's field 169
Auchenhìll—G. *achadh na chuill* (hwill), field of the wood or of the hazel-bush 105, 106
Auchenmànister—G. *achadh na manaisdir*, field of the monastery 176
Auchenrèe—? G. *achadh an fhraeich* (ree), heather field . 116
Auchenròcher — G. *achadh an chrochadhair* (hrogher), hangman's hill 170
Auchenshùgle—G. *achadh an seagail* (shaggul), rye field . 118
Auchenvèy—G. *achadh na bheith* (aha na vey), birch field 109
Auchinlèck—G. *achadh na leac* (leck), field of flagstones . 133
Auchlày ⎫
Auchleàch ⎬ G. *achadh laogh* (leuh), calves' field 125, 126
Auchlèe ⎭
Auchmànnoch—G. *achadh manach*, monk's field . . 177
Auchnagàtt—G. *achadh na' cat*, field of the wild cats . 128
Auchnashàlloch—G. *achadh na' saileach*, willow field . 119
Aùchness—G. *each inis*, horse-pasture . . . 89
Auchtralùre—G. *uachdarach lobhair* (lure), leper's upland 65
Auchtrievàne—G. *uachdarach bhán*, white upland . 65
Auld Tàggart—G. *allt shagairt* (taggart), priest's glen . 18

Index of Place-Names.

Avon—G. *amhuinn* (avon), a river 8, 79
Awhìrk—G. *achadh chuirc* (aha hwirk), oat-field . . 118
Awn—G. *amhuinn* (avon), a river 8
Ayr—N. *eyrr*, the beach 87

Baile-Uilph—G., Olaf's farm 82
Balàrgus—G. *baile Fhearguis* (argus), Fergus's croft . 62
Balfòur—G. *baile fuar*, cold place . . . 16, 62, 92
Balglàsso—G. *baile glasaich*, croft of green land . . 62
Balgòwn—G. *baile gobhain* (gowan), smith's croft . . 62
Balgràcie—G. *baile greusaich*, cobbler's house . . 169
Balkèerie—G. *baile caora*, sheep-croft . . . 62
Ballantràe—G. *baile an traigh*, farm or village on the shore 86
Ballintèer—G. *baile an t-shaoir* (teer), the carpenter's house 42
Bàllo } G. *bealach* (ballagh), a pass, a ford, a road . 160
Bàlloch }
Ballochabèastie—G. *bealach na' biasta*, pass of the cattle . 160
Ballochalèe, G. *bealach na' laogh*, pass of the calves 126, 160
Ballymènach } G. *baile meadhonach* (mennoch), middle
Balmìnnoch } house, Middleton 177
Balmùick—G. *baile muic*, swine-farm . . . 123
Balnàb—G. *baile an aib*, abbot's house . . . 177
Balnòwlart—G. *baile n' ubhal ghart* (owlhart), apple-yard farm 137
Balsàggart—G. *baile sagart*, house of the priests . 44, 177
Balshère } G. *baile saoir* (seer), carpenter's house ; or *baile*
Balsìer } *siar* (shere), west house . . . 169
Baltìer—G. *baile t-shaoir* (teer), the carpenter's house ; or *baile t-iar* (teer), west house . . . 42, 169
Barbèth—G. *barr bethach* (beyagh), birchwood-hill . 109
Bardràin—G. *barr draighean*, blackthorn-hill . . 114
Bardrìshach—G. *barr drìsach* (drissagh), bramble-hill . 114
Bardròch Wood—G. *barr drochid*, bridge hill . . 19

Index of Place-Names. 187

Barglàss—G. *barr glas*, green top . . . 10, 15
Barhòise (pron. Barhòsh)—G. *barr os* (osh), hill of the fawns; or *barr shuas* (hosh), upper or north hill . 121
Barhùllion—G. *barr chuilean*, hill of the whelps . . 101
Barlaè—G. *barr laogh* (leuh), calves' hill . . . 125
Barlàuchlane—G. *barr Lochlinn*, the Norsemen's hill . 91
Barlaùgh—G. *barr laogh* (leuh), calves' hill . . . 125
Barlòckhart—G. *barr luachair*, rushy hill; or *barr lucairt*, hill of the big house 117
Barlùel—G. *barr llamh chuill* (lav whill), hill-top of the elm-wood 111
Barlùre—G. *barr lobhar* (lure), leper's hill . . . 170
Barnagèe—G. *bearna gaoithe* (geuha, gwee), windy pass; or *barr na gaoithe*, windy hill . . . 84, 159
Barnamòn—G. *barr nam ban* (*b* eclipsed), hill-top of the women 145
Barnbàuchle—G. *bearna bocghail*, gap of danger, or *buachail*, shepherd's gap 159
Barnbòard—G. *barr na' bard*, hill-top of the poets . 168
Barncàlzie (*z*=*y*)—G. *barr na cailleaich*, hill-top of the woman, witch, or nun 145
Barncròsh—G. *barr an crois*, gallows-hill . . . 170
Barnecàllagh—G. *barr na cailleaich*, hill-top of the woman, witch, or nun 145
Barneyclèary—G. *barr na clerech*, hill of the clergy . 177
Barneywàter—G. *bearna uachdar*, upper pass . . 145
Barnkìrk ⎫ G. *barr an coirce* (curk, curkia), hill of the
Barnkìrky ⎭ oats 75, 118
Barnsàllie—G. *barr na saileach*, willow-hill . . . 112
Barnshàlloch—G. *barr an sealghe* (shallogh), hill of the hunting 112, 119
Barr—G. *barr*, a hill-top 144
Barràer—G. *barr air*, hill of the slaughter, or of the ploughing 39

Index of Place-Names.

Barsàlloch—G. *barr saileach*, willow-hill . . . 112
Barskeòch—G. *barr sgitheog* (skeog), hawthorn-hill . 113
Bartàggart—G. *barr t-shagairt* (taggart), hill-top of the priest 44, 177
Barwhìll—G. *barr chuill* (hwill), hill-top of the wood, or of the hazel bush 105, 106
Barwhìrran—G. *barr chaoruinn* (hearrun), rowan-tree hill 112
Beàrholm—A.S. *bere holm*, barley-field . . . 94
Beàrsden—A.S. *bár denn*, wild boar's lair . . . 123
Beàryards—A.S. *bere garth*, barley-yard . . . 94
Beith—? G. *beith*, birch-tree 109
Bellybòcht—G. *baile bochd*, poor man's house . . 170
Ben Macdhùi—G. *beinn muic duibhe* (dooey), hill of the black sow 124
Benbòwie—G. *beinn buidhe* (buie), yellow horn or headland 139
Bengrày—G. *beinn gréaich*, hill of the high flat, or *graich*, of the horse-drove 139
Benmòre—G. *beinn mòr*, great hill 15
Bènnan—G. *beinnán*, a hill 139
Bennanbràck—G. *beinnán breac*, dappled hill . . 139
Bennùskie—G. *beinn uisce*, horn or rock in the water . 139
Bènny—G. *beinnach*, horned, a hilly place . . . 139
Benshàlag—G. *beinn sealghe* (shallogh), hill-face of the hunting 119
Bentùdor—G. *beinn t-shudaire* (tudory), tanner's hill . 169
Benyèllary—G. *beinn iolaire* (yillary), eagle's hill . 96, 139
Bèoch—G. *beitheach* (beyagh), birch-land . . . 109
Bèrnera—N. *Björnar ey*, Björn's island . . . 91
Bidean-a'-ghlas-thuill (a-hlass-hule) — G. pinnacle of the green hollow 158, 164
Bìggar ⎫
Bìggart ⎬ N. *bygg garðr*, barley-field . . . 94
Bìggarts ⎭
Bìggins—A.S. *byggan*, building 95

Index of Place-Names. 189

Bìgholm—N. *bygg holmr*, barley-land . . . 94
Bìrket—A.S. *beorc wudu*, birch-wood . . 107, 109
Bìrkshaw—A.S. *beorc scaga*, birch-wood . . . 107
Blàiket—A.S. *blæc wudu*, black wood . . . 107
Blair—G. *blár*, a plain, a field 10, 134
Blairdàff—G. *blár damh* (dav), ox-field . . . 125
Blairgòwan ⎫ G. *blár gobhan* (gowan), smith's field; or
Blairingònè ⎭ *gamhan* (gowan), calves' field . 168, 169
Blairhòsh—G. *blár shuas* (hosh), upper field . . 134
Blairmàkin—G. *blár meacan* (maakan), field of the roots
 (carrots, &c.) 118
Blairmòddie—G. *blár madadh* (madduh), wolf's field . 126
Blairnàirn—G. *blár n' fhearn* (nern), alder-field . . 135
Blairninìch—G. *blár nan each*, horse-field . . . 135
Blairquhàn—G. *blár Chon*, Conn's field, or the dog's field 127
Blairshìnnoch—G. *blár sionach* (shinnagh), fox-field . 135
Blawràiny—G. *blár raithneach* (rahnah), ferny plain . 115
Bochàstle—G. *both chaisteail*, hut or croft of the castle . 63
Bòllsa ⎫
Bòsta ⎬ N. *bólstaðr*, a farmhouse or dwelling . . 92
Boust ⎪
Bùsta ⎭
Bonèen—G. *bunín*, a little rump 162
Bonèssan—G. *bun easain* (assan), foot of the waterfall . 162
Bootle—A.S. *botl*, a house or dwelling . . . 62
Boquhàn—G. *both Chon*, Conn's hut, or the dog's hut . 127
Bòreland—O.N.E. *bord land*, ground kept for the maintenance of the chief house 123
Bòrestone, a pierced stone (cf. Thirlestane) . . . 123
Bòwhill—? G. *buachaill*, a boy or herd, *fig.* a solitary stone 158
Bòwling—G. *bo linn*, cow-pool 125
Bràco—? G. *bréagh mhagh* (brā vah), wolf-field . 39, 127
Bràdock—G. *braghadach* (braadagh), the throat, a gulley 148
Braemòre—G. *braigh mór*, great brae . . . 147

Index of Place-Names.

Braid Hills, The—G. *braghad* (braad), the breast . . 148
Breadàlban—G. *braghad Albainn*, the breast or upland of Scotland 148
Brèaklet—N. *breiða klettr*, broad cliff . . . 88
Brèddock—G. *braghadach* (braadagh), the throat, a gulley 148
Breedie Burn—G. (*allt*) *Brighde*, St Bride's stream . 175
Breich—G. *braigh*, a top or summit 147
Bròadford—N. *breiðr fjörðr*, broad firth . . 83, 90
Bròcket—A.S. *brocc wudu*, badger-wood . . . 128
Bròcklees—A.S. *brocc leah*, badger-field . . . 128
Bròckloch—G. *broclach*, a badger-warren . . . 128
Bròckwoodlees — O.N.E. *brocc wode lea*, field of the badger-wood 129
Bròdick—N. *breiðr vík*, broad bay 84
Brough—G. *bruach*, a brae, or *borg, brog, brugh*, a house . 148
Bròxburn—O.N.E. *brocces burn*, badger-stream . . 129
Bùckhurst—O.N.E. *bucce hurst*, wood of the fallow buck 122
Bugle Ètive—G. *buachaill*, a boy or herd—*i.e.*, a solitary hill 158
Buittle—A.S. *botl*, a house, a dwelling-place . . 62
Bunàwe—G. *bun Amh* (aw), foot of Loch Awe . . 162
Buttanlòin—G. or P. *butt an loin*, marsh croft . . 63
Buttcùrry—G. or P. *butt curaich*, moor or marsh croft . 63
Buttdùbh—G. or P. *butt dubh*, black croft . . . 63
Buttnacòille—G. or P. *butt na coille*, wood croft . . 63
Buttnacrèig—G. or P. *butt na' creag*, croft of the crags . 63
Buttnamàdda—G. or P. *butt nam madadh* (maddah), croft of the wolves or dogs 63
Bùxburn—O.N.E. *bucces bourne*, stream of the fallow buck 122

Caerlàverock—G. *cathair* (caher) *leamhreaich* (lavrah), fortress in the elm-wood 111
Cairngòrm—G. *carn gorm*, blue cairn or hill . . 154
Cairntòul—G. *carn tuathal* (tual), north cairn or hill . 154

Index of Place-Names. 191

Càithness—P. *Cata*, N. *nes*, the promontory of Cait   58, 89
Càlbost—N. *kald bólstaðr*, cold croft 92
Càldons—G. *calltunn*, hazels 106
Calf of Man, the—G. *an Calbh Manannach*, N. *Manarkalfr*   4
Cambusnèthan — G. *camus Nèthan*, bend of the river
    Nethan 117
Càmelon—G. *cam linn*, winding pool 171
Càmisk—G. *cam uisce*, winding water . . . 171
Càmisky—G. *cam uisce*, winding water . . . 171
Càmple Burn—G. *cam pol*, winding water . . . 171
Càmpsie—? A.S. *campsted*, a battle-field . . . 136
Cantỳre—G. *ceann tír*, head of the land, land's end . 131
Carlìsle—W. *caer Lliwelydd*, Lliwelydd's stronghold . 16
Carlùre—G. *ceathramh lobhar* (carrow lure), leper's land-
    quarter 171
Carmìnnow—G. *ceathramh monaidh* (carrow munney),
    moorland quarter 168
Carnèltoch—G. *carn eilte* (elty), hind's cairn or hill . 120
Càrrick—G. *caraig*, W. *careg*, a crag . . . 50, 155
Carstàirs—W. *caer Terras*, Terras's fortress . . . 16
Cart (river)—G. *caraid*, a pair 16
Castle Creavie—G. *caiseal craebhe*, castle of the tree . 107
Castle Shell—G. *caiseal sealghe* (shalluh), hunting-tower . 119
Castràmont—G. *cas tromain*, foot of the elder-bush . 112
Càtgill—N. *kattr gil*, wild cat's ravine . . . 128
Cathcàrt—G. *cathair* (caher) *Cairt*, fortress on the river
    Cart 16
Càttadale—N. *kattr dalr*, wild cat's dale . . . 128
Càven } G. *cabhan* (cavvan), a hollow . . . 161
Càvens }
Chàlloch—G. *tealach* (tyallagh), forge . . 119, 169
Chester, Chesters—L. *castrum*, a camp . . . 28
Chipperdàndy—G. *tiobar shaint* (hant) *Antoin*, St An-
    thony's well 176

Index of Place-Names.

Chipperdìngan—G. *tiobar Dingain*, St Ninian's well	172
Chipperfìnian—G. *tiobar Finain*, St Finan's well	176
Chipperhèron—G. *tiobar Chiarain*, St Kieran's well	176
Clàchaig—G. *clacheach*, a stony place	158
Clàchan—G. *clachean*, stones, hence a hamlet	158
Clachanamùck—G. *clachan nam muc*, stones of the swine	123
Clàchog—G. *clachóg*, a small stone	158
Clàchrie—G. *clachreach*, a stony place	158
Clàchrum—G. *clacherín*, a stony place	158
Clàckrie—G. *clachreach*, a stony place	158
Claddiochdòw—G. *claddach dubh* (doo), black shore	87
Clàdy House—G. *claddach*, the shore or beach	87
Clamdàlly—G. *claon* (clan) *dealghe* (dallig), thorn-slope	115
Clamdìsh—G. *claen dess*, southern slope	154
Clànerie—G. *claenrach*, sloping land	83
Clànnoch—G. *claenach*, sloping ground	153
Clantibùies—G. *cluainte buidhe* (buie), yellow meadows	164
Clànyard—G. *claen ard*, sloping height	154
Clàry—G. *clerech*, the clergy	177
Clàttranshaws—N. *klettr*, a cliff; M.E. *shaw*, a wood	88
Clàuchrie—G. *clachreach*, a stony place	158
Claymòddie, formerly Glenmaddie,—G. *gleann madadh* (madduh), wolf's glen	126
Clayshànt—G. *clach seant* (*shant*), holy stone	157
Clean—G. *claen*, a slope	153
Clènarie ⎫ G. *claenrach*, sloping land Clèndrie ⎭	83, 153
Clene—G. *claen*, a slope	153
Clènnoch—G. *claenach*, sloping ground	154
Clènries—G. *claenreach*, sloping ground	153
Clènter—G. *claen tír*, sloping ground	154
Clòintie—G. *cluainte*, the meadows	164
Clone—G. *cluan*, a meadow	164
Clonfìn—G. *cluan fionn*, white meadow	164

Index of Place-Names.

Clonròad—G. *cluan ramhfhoda* (rah-oda), meadow of the boat-race	25
Clonskèa—G. *cluan sgitheach* (skeagh), hawthorn-meadow	164
Clorìddrick—G. *cloch Riddeirch*, stone of Ryderch (Hael)	157
Clune—G. *cluan*, a meadow	164
Clùtag—G. *clitag*, eighth part of a penny-land . .	167
Clyne—G. *claen*, a slope	153
Colintràive—G. *caol an t-shnaoimh* (trave), strait of the swimming	42
Còngalton, formerly Cnoccomgall—G. *cnoc Comgall*, hill of the Comgall or Frisians; A.S. *tún*, added .	70
Connemàra—G. *Conmaicne mara*, the sea-side progeny of Conmac	41
Còpeval—N. *kupu fjall*, cup-shaped hill . . .	88
Còran } G. *corán*, a round hill	157
Còrran }	
Core Hill—G. *cor*, a round hill, or *cathair* (caher), a camp	157
Còrnabus—N. *korn bólstaðr*, corn-farm . . .	92
Corncràvie—G. *corán craobhach* or *craove*, wooded hill .	107
Cornlèe—G. *corán liath* (lee), grey hill . . .	157
Corra Linn—G. *coire*, a caldron or kettle . . .	162
Corra Pool (Kirkcudbright Dee)—G. *coradh* (corra), a fish-weir	162
Corriefècklach—G. *coire feocalach*, polecat's corrie .	129
Corròur—G. *coire odhar* (corry our), grey or dun corrie .	23
Còrsbie—N. *krosa by*, cross-house	91
Corvìsel (pron. Corvèezle)—G. *coire iseal* (eeshal), low pool	162
Còwan—G. *cabhan* (cavvan), a hollow . . .	161
Cràchan—G. *cruachán*, a hill	150
Cràggan—G. *creagean*, the crags, or *creagán*, a little crag	155
Craichmòre—G. *cruach mór*, great hill . . .	150
Craigbènnoch—G. *creag beinnach*, horned crag . .	139
Craigbèrnoch—G. *creag bearnach*, cloven crag . .	159
Craigencàt—G. *creagan cat*, wild cat's crag . . .	128

194 Index of Place-Names.

Craigendòran—G. *creag an dorain*, otter's rock . . 128
Craigenfèoch ⎫ G. *creagán fiadh* (feeah), deer-crags, or
Craigenvèoch ⎭   *fitheach* (feeah), raven-crags . 43, 120
Cràigie—G. *creagach*, craggy, rocky 155
Craiginèe—G. *creag an fhiaidh* (ee), the deer's crag . 120
Craiglèe—G. *creag liath* (lee), grey crag . . . 126
Craiglèy—G. *creag laogh* (leuh), calves' ridge . . 126
Craiglùre—G. *creag lobhair* (lure), leper's crag . . 170
Craignafèoch—G. *creag na fithach* (feeah), raven-crags . 120
Craignèlder—G. *creag n'eilte* (elty), hind's crag . . 120
Craignìsh—O.G. *creag an ois* (ish), the fawn's crag . 121
Craigò'er ⎫ G. *creag odhar* (owr), grey crag ; or *creag*
Craigòver ⎭   *gobhar* (gowr), goat's crag . . . 22
Craigslàve—G. *creag sleamh* (slav), elm-crag . . 111
Craigsloùan—G. *creag slamhain* (slavvan), elm-crag . 111
Cràilloch—G. *crithlach* (creelagh), a shaking bog . . 164
Cràmond—G. *cathair* (caher) *amuin*, fortress on the river 8
Cràwick—W. *caer Rywc*, Rawic's fortress . . . 14
Creag Leacach—G. crag of the flagstones, or sloping crag 154
Crèechan—? G. *criothachean* (creeghan), aspens . 110, 150
Creich—G. *criothach* (creeagh), the aspen . . . 110
Cretanrèe—G. *croit an fhraeich* (ree), heather-croft . 116
Crianlàrich—G. *crich* or *criothach* (creeagh) *na laraich*,
    boundary or aspen-tree at the house-site . . 110
Crieff—? G. *criothach* (creeagh), aspen . . . 110
Crìffel—N. *kráka fjall*, crow-hill 88
Croach—G. *cruach*, a stack, a hill 150
Cròachy—G. *cruachach*, a hilly place . . . 150
Cròchan—G. *cruachán*, a hill 150
Crochmòre—G. *cruach mór*, great hill . . . 150
Crochrìoch—G. *cnoc riabhach* (reeagh), streaked hill . 41
Crockencàlly—G. *crochan cailleach*, nun's hillock . . 40
Cròssapool—N. *krosa bólstaðr*, croft of the cross . . 92
Crùchie—G. *cruachach*, a hilly place 150
Crùivie—G. *craobhach* (creuvagh), wooded . . . 107

Index of Place-Names.

Crỳla—G. *crithlach* (creelagh), a shaking bog . . 164
Cuff Hill—? W. *cefn* (kevn), a ridge 51
Cuil—G. *cuil*, a corner 161
Cuildrỳnach—G. *cúl, cuil,* or *coill draighneach* (dreinagh),
    the hill-back, corner, or wood of the blackthorns . 161
Culbràtten—G. *cúl Breatain*, hill-back of the Welshmen 46, 67
Culdèrry—G. *cúl doire* (dìrry), back of the wood . . 108
Culdòch—G. *cúl dabhaich* (dawgh), back of the salmon-weir 166
Culhòrn—G. *cuil eorn* (yorn), corner of the barley . 118
Culkàe—G. *cúl caedha* (kay), back of the bog . . 163
Cùllen—G. *coillín*, woodland 106
Cullòden—G. *cúl lodain*, back of the swamp . . 164
Culmàddie—G. *cuil madadh* (madduh), wolf's corner . 126
Culmòre—G. *coill mór*, great wood . . . 105, 161
Culquhìrk—G. *cuil chuirc* (hwirk), corner of the oats . 118
Culràin—G. *cuil rathain* (rahen), corner of the ferns . 161
Culròy—G. *cúl ruadh* (rooa), red-hill back . . . 160
Culscàdden—G. *cuil scadan*, corner of the herrings . 161
Cult—G. *coillte*, the woods 106
Cultmìck—*G. coillte muic*, swine-woods . . . 106
Cults—G. *coillte*, the woods 106
Cultùllich—G. *cúl tulaich*, back of the hill . . . 106
Cumlòden } G. *cam lodain*, bend of the swamp . . 164
Cumlòdden }
Cùmnock—*cam cnoc*, bent hill 140
Curleywèe—G. *cor le gaeith* (geuh, gwee), hill in the wind 157
Curnèlloch—? G. *cor n'eilidh* (elly), hill of the hinds . 157
Cùrrah } O.G. *currach*, a marsh 163
Cùrrie }
Cuttyshàllow—G. *ceide sealghe* (keddy shalluh), hill-brow
    of the hunting 119

Dailly—G. *dealghe* (dalhy), the thorns . . . 115
Dalintòbar—G. *dal an tiobair*, land of the well . . 99
Dally—G. *dealghe* (dalhy), the thorns . . . 115

196 Index of Place-Names.

Dalnacàrdoch—G. *dal na ceardaich*, land of the smithy . 99
Dalnadàmph—G. *dal na' damh* (dav), ox-land . . 125
Dalnaspìdal—G. *dal na spidail*, land of the hospital . 99
Dalriàda—G. *dal righe fhada* (ree ahda), land of (Cairbre with) the long arm ; or *dal righ fhada*, land of the tall king (Cairbre) 98
Dalrỳ—G. *dal righ*, king's land 99
Dalrymple — G. *dal chruim puill*, land of the curving pool 88, 99
Darnàrbel—G. *dobhar* (dour) *an earbuill*, water of the tail (cf. Grey Mare's Tail) 163
Dàrra—G. *darach*, an oak 108
Dàrroch—G. *darach*, an oak 108
Dàvo—G. *dabhach*, a davach (a measure of land) . . 165
Davochbèg—G. *dabhach beag*, little davach . . . 165
Davochfin—G. *dabhach fionn*, white davach . . 165
Deer—O.G. *daur*, an oak 108
Delòrain (*not* Dĕlŏrain)—G. *dal Orain*, Oran's land . 17
Dèrry—G. *doire*, an oak wood, a wood . . 108, 109
Dèvon (river)—G. *dubh amhuinn* (doo avon), black water 172
Dìngwall—N. *þinga völlr*, the assembly field . . 89
Dìnnance
Dìnnans
Dìnning
Dìnnings
G. *dúnan*, the hills or forts, the downs . 159
Dìpple—G. *dubh* (doo) *pol*, black water . . 100, 171
Dirriemòre—G. *doire* (dìrry) *mór*, great wood . . 109
Dirvàird—G. *dobhur* (dour) or *doire* (dirry) *bhaird* (vaird), the bard's water or wood 106
Dochfòur—G. *dabhach fuar*, cold davach (a measure of land) 165
Dochgàrroch—G. *dabhach garbh* (davach garriv), rough davach 165
Doon—G. *dubh amhuinn* (doo awn), black river . 100, 171
Dòuglas—G. *dubh* (doo) *glas*, black water . 15, 100, 171

Index of Place-Names.

Dòwnan—G. *dúnan*, a hill or fort 159
Dràinie—G. *draighneach* (drānah), place of blackthorns . 114
Drangòwer—G. *draigheanan gobhar* (drannan gowr), blackthorns of the goats 114
Drannandòw—G. *draighnean dubh* (doo), dark blackthorns 114
Dranniemànner—G. *draighean na mainir*, blackthorns at the goat-pen 114
Drem—G. *druim*, a ridge 10, 142
Drimnasàllie—G. *druim na saileach*, willow-ridge . . 112
Drìsaig—G. *drisach* (drissah), a place of brambles . . 114
Dròch Head—G. *drochaid*, a bridge 18
Dromòre—G. *druim mór*, great ridge 142
Dron—G. *draighean*, blackthorns 114
Drònach—G. *draighneach* (drānah), place of blackthorns . 114
Drònnan—G. *draighnean*, blackthorns . . . 114
Drum—G. *druim*, a ridge 10, 142
Drumanèe—G. *druim an fhiaidh* (ee), the deer's ridge . 120
Drumavàird—G. *druim a' bhaird* (vaird), rhymer's hill . 168
Drumbàe—G. *druim beith* (bey), birch-hill . . . 109
Drumbòw—G. *druim bo*, cow-ridge 125
Drumbrèddan—G. *druim Breatain*, Welshman's hill 46, 67
Drumdàlly—G. *druim dealg* (dallig), thorn-ridge . . 115
Drumdrìsaig—G. *druim drisach* (drissagh), bramble-ridge 114
Drumèarnachan—G. *druim fhearnachain*, ridge of the alder-wood or of the sloes 111
Drumfàrnachan—G. *druim fearnachan*, ridge of the alder-wood or of the sloes 111
Drumlànrig—G. *druim*, a ridge, W. *llanerch*, a clearing in a forest 50
Drumlèan—G. *druim lín* (leen), flax-ridge . . . 118
Drumlèy—G. *druim laogh* (leuh), calves' ridge . . 126
Drumlòckhart—G. *druim luachair*, rushy ridge; or *druim lucairt*, ridge of the big house 117
Drumlòur—G. *druim lobhar* (lure), leper's ridge . . 170

198   *Index of Place-Names.*

Drummatìer—G. *druim a' t-shaoir* (teer), the carpenter's ridge 41, 169
Drummòddie—G. *druim madadh* (madduh), wolf's ridge . *126
Drummòre—G. *druim mór*, great ridge . . . 142
Drummùck—G. *druim muc*, swine-ridge . . . 123
Drummùckloch—G. *druim muclaich*, ridge of the swine pasture 124
Drumnamìnshog—G. *druim nam uinnseog* (inshog), ash-tree ridge 110
Drumnàrbuck—G. *druim an earbuic*, roebuck's ridge . 122
Drumòver—G. *druim odhar* (our), grey ridge . . 23
Drumràe—O.G. *druim raith* (ray), fern-ridge . . 115
Drumràny—G. *druim raithneach* (rahnah), fern-ridge . 115
Drumshàlloch—G. *druim sealghe* (shalluh), hunting ridge 119
Drumsheùgh—G. *druim sealghe* (shalluh), hunting ridge . 119
Drumskeòg—G. *druim sgitheog* (skeog), hawthorn-hill . 113
Drumtùrk—G. *druim tuirc*, wild boar's ridge . . 123
Drumvòre—G. *druim mhór* (vore), great ridge . . 142
Drùngan—G. *draighnean*, blackthorns . . . 114
Drỳmen (Drìmmen)—G. *dromán*, a ridge . . 10, 142
Drỳnach ⎫
Drỳnie ⎬ same as Drònach, *q.v.* 114
Drỳnachan—G. *draighneachán*, place of blackthorns . 114
Dùart—G. *dubh ghart* (doo hart), black paddock . . 137
Duisk—G. *dubh* (doo) *uisce*, black water . . . 171
Dumbàrton—G. *dún Bretann*, the Welshmen's fortress . 35
Dumfrìes   G. *dún Fris*, the Frisians' fortress . . . 72
Duncrùb—O.G. *dún craeb*, hill of the trees . . . 159
Dundrènnan—G. *dún draighnean*, blackthorn hill or fort 114
Dunèaton—G. *dún aitten*, juniper-hill . . . 117
Dunèdin (Edinburgh)—G. *dún Aidain*, Aidan's or Edwin's fortress 13
Dunglàs—G. *dún glas*, green hill 15
Dusk—G. *dubh* (doo) *uisc*, black water . . . 100

Index of Place-Names.   199

Eàglesfield—G. *eaglais,* W. *eglwys,* church (field) . . 29
Eàglesham—G. *eaglais,* W. *eglwys,* church (*ham,* house) . 29
Ecclefèchan—G. *eaglais Fechain,* St Vigean's church 29, 175
Eccles—G. *eaglais,* W. *eglwys,* a church . . . 28
Eden—G. *aodann,* the forehead, brow of a hill . . 150
Edendàrroch—G. *aodann darach,* hill-brow of the oaks . 151
Edinbèg—G. *aodann beag,* little hill-brow . . . 151
Edinbèlly—G. *aodann baile,* hill-brow of the farm . 151
Edinkìllie—G. *aodann coille* (kulyie), hill-brow of the wood 151
Èlderslie ⎱
Èllerslie ⎰ A.S. *alr leah,* alder-field 112
Èllerbeck—N. *ölr bekkr,* or A.S. *alr becc,* alder-brook 90, 112
Ennis—G. *inis,* waterside pasture 25
Eòrabus—N. *eyrar bólstaðr,* shore farm . . . 92
Ernànity—G. *earrann annuid,* church-land . . . 136
Ernèspie—G. *earrann espuig,* bishop's land . . . 136
Ernfìllan—G. *earrann Fillain,* Fillan's land . . . 136
Europa Point—N. *eyrar by,* beach village . . . 19
Evan—G. *amhuinn* (avon), a river 9
Eye (river)—N. *á,* a river 86

Fàirfield—N. *fœr fjall,* sheep-fell 22
Fàirgirth—N. *fœr garðr,* sheep-fold 22
Fair Isle ⎱
Fàray ⎰ N. *fœr ey,* sheep-island 22
Falbàe—G. *phol beith* (bey), birch-stream . . . 67
Fàrnoch—G. *fearnach,* place of alders . . . 111
Fàroe—N. *fœr eyjar,* sheep-islands 22
Feàrnoch ⎫
Fèrnaig ⎬ G. *fearnach,* place of alders . . . 111
Fèrnie ⎭
Ferintòsh—G. *fearann toisich,* thane's land . . . 136
Fèrnan—G. *fearnan,* alders 111

Index of Place-Names.

Fettercàirn—P. *pett an cairn*, cairn-croft . . . 64
Fìdra—N. *Boitter ey*, island of Boitter . . 71, 78
Fife—P. *Fib*, said to be one of the seven sons of Cruidne 58
Fìnglas—G. *fionn glas*, white water 171
Finhàven—P. *pett an amhuinn*, river-croft . . 64, 68
Fìnlas—G. *fionn glas*, white water 171
Fìntray—G. *fionn traigh*, white strand . . . 68
Flàdda—N. *flatr ey*, flat-isle 83
Fòrres ⎫
Forse ⎬ N. *fors*, a waterfall 93
Forss ⎪
Foss   ⎭
Frèuchie—G. *fraochach* (freughah), a heathery place . 116
Freugh ⎫ G. *fraoch* (freugh), heather 115
Frew   ⎭

Gàdgirth—N. *geit garðr*, goat-pen 22
Gàlloway—G. *gall Gaidheal* (gale), W. *Galwyddel* (Galwithel), the stranger Gaels 5, 72
Gàrioch—G. *garbh* (garriv) *achadh*, rough field . . 133
Gàrland Burn—G. *garbh* (garriv) *linn*, rough pool . . 171
Gàrnaburn—W. *afon gwernach*, alder-stream . . 47
Gàrnock (river)—W. *afon gwernach*, alder-stream . . 46
Gàrple ⎫ G. *garbh pol*, rough water 171
Gàrpol ⎭
Gàrrabost—N. *Geirra bólstaðr*, Geir's farm . . . 92
Gàrrald ⎫
Gàrrel ⎬ G. *garbh* (garriv) *allt*, rough glen or stream . 171
Gàrvald ⎪
Gàrvel ⎭
Garriefàd—G. *garadh* (garra) *fada*, long garden . . 138
Gàrry (river)—G. (*amhuinn*) *garbh* (garriv), rough river 138, 171
Gartclòss ⎫ G. *gart clois* (closhe), paddock of the trench
Gartclùsh ⎭ or ditch 137

Index of Place-Names.

Garth—G. *gart*, or N. *garðr*, an enclosure, a yard .	137
Gartnanìch—G. *gart nan each*, horse-paddock .	137
Gartnèss—G. *gart nan eas*, paddock at the waterfalls	89
Gartshèrrie—G. *gart searrach* (sharragh), colt's paddock .	138
Gartùrk—G. *gart tuirc*, boar's paddock .	138
Gartwhìnnie—G. *gart fheannagh*, enclosure of the lazy beds	138
Gàrvock—G. *garbh* (garriv) *achadh*, rough field .	134
Gàrwachy—G. *garbh* (garriv) *achadh*, rough field .	134
Garwòling—G. *garadh* (garra) *feorlin*, farthing-garden .	167
Gàteheugh—N. *geit hou*, goat-height .	22
Gàtehope—N. *geit hof*, goat-shelter .	22
Gìffen—W. *cefn* (kevn), a ridge .	51
Gillèspie—G. *cill easpuig*, bishop's chapel .	29, 177
Glack } Glaik } G. *glac*, the palm of the hand, a hollow .	160
Glàister—G. *glas tír*, green land .	15, 131
Glàssert—G. *glas ghart* (hart), green paddock .	137
Glàsserton—G. *glas ghart* (hart), green paddock, with A.S. *tún* .	131
Glàster Law—G. *glas tír*, green land ; M.E. *law*, a hill, added .	15, 131
Glàsvein—G. *glas bheinn* (ven), green hill .	15
Glàzert—G. *glas ghart* (hart), green paddock .	137
Glenàlmond—O.G. *gleann amuin*, glen of the river .	7
Glenamùckloch—G. *gleann na muclaich*, glen of the swine pasture .	124
Glenàpp—G. *gleann Alpin*, Alpin's glen .	178
Glenàrbuck—G. *gleann earboc*, glen of the roebucks .	122
Glenbùck—G. *gleann buic*, glen of the he-goat or roebuck	122
Glencàird—G. *gleann ceaird*, tinker's glen .	169
Glenchàmber—G. *gleann saimir* (shammer), clover-glen .	116
Glendòwran—G. *gleann doran*, otter-glen .	
Glendrìssock—G. *gleann drisach* (drissah), bramble-glen .	114
Glen Fìddich—? P. *gleann Fidaich*, Fidach's glen .	58

Index of Place-Names.

Glengỳre—G. *gleann gaothair* (gaiur), greyhound's glẹn . 128
Glenhòise—O.G. *gleann os* (osh), glen of the fawns; or
   G. *gleann shuas* (hosh), upper or north glen . . 121
Glenlìng—G. *gleann lín* (leen), flax-glen . . . 118
Glenlòchar—G. *gleann luachair*, rushy glen . . 117
Glenòse—O.G. *gleann os* (osh), glen of the fawns; or G.
   gleann shuas (hosh), upper or northern glen . . 121
Glenòver—G. *gleann odhar* (owr), grey glen . . 23
Glenshàlloch—G. *gleann sealghe* (shalluh), hunting-glen . 119
Glenshàmrock ⎱ G. *gleann seamrog* (shamrog), clover-
Glenshìmerock ⎰   glen 116
Glenshèllach—G. *gleann sealghe* (shalluh), hunting-glen . 119
Glenstòckadale—G. *gleann*, N. *stokkr dalr*, glen of the
   dale of the stakes or stumps 100
Glentàggart—G. *gleann t-shagairt* (taggart), priest's glen . 100
Glentùrk—G. *gleann tuirc*, wild-boar's glen . . . 123
Glenùre—G. *gleann iubhar* (yure), glen of the yews 37, 113
Glenvèrnoch—G. *gleann bhearnach* (vernagh), cloven glen 159
Gòlspie—G. *cill espuig*, bishop's chapel . . . 177
Gòrbals—? N. *görr balkr*, built walls 95
Gortinanàne—G. *gortín nan én* (ane), birds' paddock . 138
Gòvan—? W. *cefn* (kevn), a ridge 51
Grànton (near Edinburgh)—A.S. *gréne dún*, green hill . 7
Gràntown-on-Spey—M.E. Grant's town . . . 7
Grèenan—G. *grianán* (greenan), a sunny place, a palace . 24
Grèenbeck—N. *grünnr bekkr*, shallow brook . . 90
Grènnan—G. *grianán*, a sunny place, a palace . . 24
Gryfe (river)—G. (*amhuinn*) *garbh* (garriv), rough stream
   138, 171
Gùisachan—G. *giuthasachan* (geusahan), fir-wood . . 113
Gùllane—G. *guallan*, a shoulder 4
Gùlvain—G. *gabhal bheinn* (gowl ven), fork of the hill . 138

Hàbost—N. *hallr bólstaðr*, sloping farm . . . 83

Index of Place-Names. 203

Hàmnavoe—N. *höfn vagr*, haven bay . . . 84
Hàrray—N. *hár ey*, high island 86
Hàrris (formerly Herrie)—N. *hár ey*, high island . . 85
Hàwick—O.N.E. *haugh wick*, town on the low pasture . 90
Hèndon—W. *hen dún*, old fort 3
Hillmabrèedia—G. *chill ma Brighde* (hill ma breedie),
    cell of our Bridget 174
Hòbkirk—F. *hóp kirkju*, church in the shelter . . 89
Hòlland } N. *hallr land*, sloping island; or *haugr land*,
Hòulland } island of the howe or hillock . . . 83

Immervòulin—G. *iomair mhuileain* (voolin), mill-ridge—
    Milrig 155
Inch } G. *inis*, gen. *innse* (inshy), meadow near water, an
Inks } island 94
Inchnadàmph—G. *inis na' damh* (dav), ox-pasture . 125
Inshaig } G. *uinnseog* (inshog), the ash-tree . 109, 110
Inshock }
Inshanks—G. *uinnsean* (inshan), ash-trees . . . 109
Inshaw—G. *uinnse* (inshy), the ash-tree . . . 109
Inshewan—G. *uinnsean* (inshan), ash-trees . . . 109
Invernèss—G. *inbher* (inver) *Ness*, mouth of the Ness . 89
Irland (in Orkney), Ireland (in Shetland)—N. *eyrr land*,
    beach island 87
Irongrày—G. *earrann graich*, land of the horse-drove . 137
Ironlòsh—G. *earrann loise* (loshe), burnt land . . 136
Ironmànnoch—G. *earrann manach*, monk's land . . 137

Kèlso—A.S. *chalc how*, chalk-hill 19
Kèlty—G. *coillte*, the woods 106
Kenmàre—G. *ceann mara*, sea-headland . . . 41
Kenvàra—G. *ceann mhara* (vāra) sea-headland . . 41
Kibberty Kìte Well—G. *tiobar tigh Cait*, well of Catherine's house 176

Index of Place-Names.

Kilbìrnie—G. *cill Birinn*, St Birrin's church . . 7
Kilbrìde—G. *cill Brighde*, St Bride's or Bridget's church 174
Kilbròcks—G. *coill broc*, badger wood . . . 129
Kilbròok—G. *coill bruic*, badger wood . . . 129
Kilchrìst—G. *cill Crioisd*, Christ church . . . 174
Kìlda, St—G. (*oilean*) *celi Dé* (*naomh*) (kelly day nave), island of the holy servants of God, the Culdees . 91
Kildàlton—*cill daltain*, church of the foster-brother (St John) 175
Kildàrroch—G. *coill darach*, oak-wood . . . 108
Kildròchat (older Kerodroched)—G. *ceathramhadh* (carrow) *an drochid*, land quarter of the bridge . . 105
Kildrùmmie—O.G. *cill, coil*, or *cíl droma*, church, wood, or back of the ridge 142
Kilhìlt—G. *coill na heilte*, hind-wood . . . 120
Killantràe (older Kerantra)—G. *ceathramhadh* (carrow) *an traigh*, land-quarter of the shore . . 92, 105
Killantrìngan—G. *cill shaint* (ant) *Ringain*, St Ninian's church . . . . ,172
Killèan—G. *cill Sheathainn* (hane), John's church . 175
Killibràkes—? O.G. *coille bréach*, wolf-wood; or G. *coille breac* (brek), parti-coloured wood . . . 127
Killiemòre—G. *coille mór*, great wood . . 105, 161
Killiewhàn—G. *coille chon*, the wood of the dogs . . 127
Killymìnshaw—G. *coille nam uinnse* (inchy), ash-wood . 110
Kilmalcòlm—G. *cill ma Coluim*, church of our Columba . 174
Kilmàrnock—G. *cill ma Ernainuig*, church of our Ernanog (diminutive of Ernan) 174
Kilmaròn ⎫
Kilmaròonock ⎬ G. *cill ma Ronuig*, church of our Ronan . 174
Kilmìchael—G. *cill Michail*, Michael's church . . 174
Kilmòrie ⎫
Kilmòry ⎬ G. *cill Muire*, Mary's church . . 105, 173
Kilnìnian—G. *cill Nennidhain*, church of Nennidius . 172

Index of Place-Names.

Kilwìnning—G. *cill Guinain*, St Finan's church . 68, 74, 175
Kinchòil—G. *cinn choill* (hoyle), at the head of the wood   45
Kindròchit } G. *cinn drochid*, at the bridge-head   . 105
Kindròught }
Kingùssie—G. *cinn giuthasaich* (geusah), at the head of
  the fir-wood 113
Kinlòch—G. *cinn locha*, at the lake-head . . 11, 12
Kìnnabus—N. *kinnar bólsaðr*, cheek-farm, at the cheek or
  side of the hill 92
Kinnèil—G. *cinn fhaill* (ale), at the wall-head . . 66
Kintàil—G. *cinn t-shael* (tale), at the head or end of the
  tide 131
Kintỳre—G. *cinn tír*, at the head of the land, land's end 131
Kinvàrra—G. *cinn mhara* (varra), at the head of the sea . 131
Kìrkapoll—N. *kirkju bólstaðr*, kirk house or farm . . 92
Kirkbrìde—A.S. *circ*, G. *Brighde*, Bride's or Bridget's
  church 174
Kìrkby or Kìrby—N. *kirkju by*, kirk town . . . 91
Kirkchrìst—A.S. *circ*, G. *Crioisd*, Christ church . . 174
Kirkcòlm—A.S. *circ*, G. *Coluim*, Columba's church . 174
Kirkcùdbright (pron. Kirkoobry) — G. *circ Cudbricht*,
  Cuthbert's kirk 75
Kirkdòminie—A.S. *circ*, L. *domini*, the Lord's church . 174
Kirkgùnzeon (pron. Kirkgunnion)—G. *circ Guinnin*, St
  Finan's church 68, 75, 175
Kìrkhope—N. *kirkju hóp*, kirk glen 89
Kirklàuchlane—G. *cathair* (caher) *Lochlinn*, Norsemen's
  fort 92
Kirkmabrèck—A.S. *circ*, G. *ma Brice* (breekie), church
  of our Brecan 174
Kirkmàiden—A.S. *circ Medainn*, Medana's church . 176
Kirkmìchael—A.S. *circ*, G. *Michail*, Michael's church . 174
Kirmìnnoch—G. *ceathramh manach* or *meadhonach* (carrow
  mennogh), monk's quarterland or middle quarterland 168

Kittyshàlloch — G. *ceide sealghe* (keddy shalluh), hill-
brow of the hunting 119, 157
Knap—G. *cnap*, a knob, hillock—N. *knappr* . . 155
Knapèrna—G. *cnap fhearna* (erna), alder-knoll . . 156
Knàppoch—G. *cnapach*, a hilly place . . . 156
Kneep } N. *gnipa*, a peak 88
Knipe, The }
Knìpoch—G. *cnapach*, a hilly place 156
Knockamàirly—G. *cnoc a' mearlaich*, thief's hill . . 170
Knockbògle—G. *cnoc buachail*, shepherd's hill . . 170
Knockcànnon—G. *cnoc ceann fhionn* (can hin), hill of the
white top 47
Knockcràvie—G. *cnoc craobhach* (creuvah) or *craobhe*,
wooded hill 107
Knockcròsh—G. *cnoc crois*, gallow's hill . . . 170
Knockenbàird—G. *cnoc an baird*, rhymer's hill . . 168
Knockenhàrry—G. *cnoc an fhaire* (harry), hill of the
watching 124
Knockentàrry—G. *cnoc an tairbhe* (tarry), bull's hill . 124
Knockgìlsie } G. *cnoc giolcach*, broom-hill . . 117
Knockgùlsha }
Knockhìlly — G. *cnoc chuille* (hwilly), hill of the
wood 140
Knockmànister—G. *cnoc manaisdir*, monastery hill . 176
Knockmàrloch—G. *cnoc mearlach*, thieves' hill . . 170
Knocknàr—G. *cnoc n'air*, hill of the slaughter, or of the
ploughing 39
Knocknìnshock—G. *cnoc na' uinnseog* (inshog), ash-tree
hill 110
Knockrèoch—G. *cnoc riabhach* (reeagh), grey hill . . 41
Knockròger—G. *cnoc chrochadhair* (hroghair), hangman's
hill 170
Knockshèllie—G. *cnoc sealghe* (shalluh), hunting-hill . 119
Knockshòggle—G. *cnoc seagail* (shaggul), rye-hill . . 118

Index of Place-Names. 207

Knockstòcks—G. *cnoc stuc*, hill of the peaks	152
Knòydart—N. *Cnuts fjörðr*, Cnut's firth	84
Làcasdle—N. *laxar dalr*, salmon-river dale	99
Lag—G. *lag*, a hollow	160
Làggan—G. *lagán*, a hollow	160
Lagniemàwn—G. *lag nam ban*, the women's hollow	43
Lagtùtor—G. *lag t-shudaire* (tudory), tanner's hollow	169
Laichtàlpine—G. *lecht Alpin*, Alpin's tomb	179
Lairg—G. *learg* (larg), a slope or hillside	149
Làkin—G. *leacán*, a hillside	153
Làmington—O.N.E. *Lambin tín*, Lambin's house	101
Lamlàsh—G. *lann mo Lais*, church of St Molio	175
Lànark—W. *llanerch*, a clearing in a forest	50
Làngavat—N. *langa vatn*, long lake	90
Langbèdholm—O.G. *lann Bedleim*, church of Bethlehem	176
Lànrick—W. *llanerch*, a clearing in a forest	50
Larg—G. *learg* (larg), a slope or hillside	149
Làrgie—G. *leargaidh* (largie), a hillside	149
Largiebèg—G. *leargaidh beag*, little hillside	149
Largiebrèak—G. *leargaidh breac*, dappled hillside	149
Largiemòre—G. *leargaidh mór*, great hillside	149
Largiewèe—G. *leargaidh bhuidh* (largie wee), yellow hillside	149
Làrgo—G. *leargaidh* (largie), a hillside	149
Largs—G. *learg* (larg), a slope or hillside	149
Largue—G. *learg* (larg), a slope or hillside	149
Largvèy—G. *learg bheith* (vey), hill-side of the birch-trees	109
Làthro—G. *latracha* (plural of *leth tír*), the slopes	150
Lauchentìlly—G. *leacán tulaich*, slope of the hill	153
Laune (river)—G. (*amhuinn*) *leamhan* (lavan, laun), elm-river	111
Làxdale—N. *laxar dalr*, salmon-river dale	100

Index of Place-Names.

Leadburn (Mid-Lothian)—G. *lec Bernard*, Bernard's or Birrin's stone	6
Lèakin—G. *leacán*, a hillside	153
Lèckie—G. *leacach*, a hillside	153
Leffinclèary—G. *leth pheighinn* (leyffin) *clereich*, parson's halfpenny-land	177
Leffindònald—G. *leth pheighinn* (leyffin) *Donuil*, Donald's halfpenny-land	167
Lefnòl—G. *leth pheighinn Amhalghaidh* (leyffin Owlhay), Olaf's or Aulay's halfpenny-land	167
Lemnamùick—G. *leum na muic*, the sow's leap	124
Lenagbòyach—G. *leana bathaich* (ba-ach), meadow of the cow-house	164
Lèndal—N. *len dalr*, fief or fee dale	86
Lènnie } Lèny } G. *leana* (lenna), a meadow	164
Lènnox—G. *leamhnach* (lavnah), elm-wood	111
Lenziebèg—G. *leana beag*, little meadow	164
Lesmahàgow—W. *eglwys Machuti*, St Machutus's church	29, 175
Lètter—G. *leth* (ley) *tír*, a hillside	149
Letterbèg—G. *leth* (ley) *tír beag*, little hillside	150
Letterdhù—G. *leth* (ley) *tír dubh*, dark hillside	150
Lettermòre—G. *leth* (ley), *tír mór*, great hillside	150
Lèttrick—G. *latracha* (plural of *leth tír*), the slopes	150
Leùcarrow—G. *leth ceathramh* (ley carrow), half-quarter land	168
Lèven—G. *leamhan* (lavan), the elms	110, 111
Lèwis—G. *leoghas*, marshy (land)	85
Lìberland—A.S. *libber land*, leper's land	170
Lìberton—A.S. *libber tún*, leper's house	170
Linclùden—W. *llyn glutvein*, pool of the Cluden	17
Lincòm—G. *linn cam*, winding pool	171
Lingàt—G. *linn cat*, wild cat's linn	128
Lìnshader—N. *lìn setr*, flax croft	93

Index of Place-Names.

Loch Conn—G. *loch Con*, Conn's lake or the dog's lake . 127
Loch Dròma—O.G. *loch droma*, lake of the ridge . . 142
Loch Goosie—G. *loch giuthasach* (geusagh), lake of the pine-wood 113
Loch Stòrnua—N. *Stjarna vágr*, Stjarna's bay; G. *loch* prefixed 90
Loch Thèalasbhaidh (pron. Hèllasvah)—N. *Hellas vágr*, Hella's bay; G. *loch* prefixed 84
Loch Vàlley—G. *loch bhealaich* (valleh), loch of the pass 134
Lòchar (river)—G. *luachair*, rushes 117
Lochenalìng—G. *lochán na lín* (leen), flax lakelet . . 118
Lochinvàr—G. *loch an bharra*, lake of the hill . . 145
Loddanmòre—G. *lodán mór*, great swamp . . . 164
Loddanrèe—G. *lodán fhraeich* (hree), heather-swamp . 164
Lòdens, The—G. *lodan*, the swamps 164
Lodnigàpple—G. *lod nan capul*, swamp of the horses . 164
Lògan—G. *lagán*, a hollow 160
Lògie—G. *lagach*, a low-lying place 160
Lòmond—G. *leaman*, the elms 110
Lòndon—W. *lon dyn* or *dún*, marsh fort, Londinium . 3
Long Maidens—O.G. *lann Medainn*, St Medana's church 176
Long Newton—W. *llan*, a church, with M.E. suffix . 49
Lòngridge (formerly Lànrig)—W. *llanerch*, a clearing in a forest 50, 74
Lòwran } G. *leamhraidhean* (lavran, lowran), elm-wood 111
Lòwring }
Lumphànan } G. *lann Finain*, Finan's church . 68, 175
Lumphìnnans }
Lune (river)—G. (*amhuinn*) *leamhan* (lavan, laun), elm-river 110
Lurg—G. *learg* (larg), a slope or hillside . . . 149
Lùrgan—G. *leargán*, a hillside 149

Màchar (parishes in Aberdeen)—G. (*eaglais*) *Machori*, St Machorius's church 12, 132

o

Index of Place-Names.

Màcher—G. *machair*, a plain or field	133
Macherakìll—G. *machaire cill* (maharry keel), kirk-field .	12
Macheràlly—G. *machair Amhalghaidh* (Owlhay), Olaf's or Aulay's field	82
Màchrie—G. *machaire* (maghery), flat land near the sea .	133
Mahàar—O.G. *magh air*, field of the ploughing, or the slaughter	133
Mambèg—G. *mam beag*, little waste	152
Mamòre—G. *mam mór*, great waste	152
Màxton—A.S. *Maccus' tún*, house of Maccus . .	180
Maxwhèel—A.S. *Maccus' wiel*, pool of Maccus . .	180
Mealgàrve—G. *meall garbh* (garriv), rough hill . .	143
Mealmòre—G. *meall mór*, great hill	143
Mearns, The—P. *magh Gìrginn*, plain of Cirig . .	58
Mèavig—N. *mjó-vágr*, narrow bay	90
Mentèith—G. *monadh Teid*, moor of the river Teith .	146
Mildrìggan—A.S. *myln*, O.G. *droigen* (dreggen), mill of Dreggan—*i.e.*, the blackthorns	113
Miljòan—G. *meall don*, brown hill	143
Mìllegan—G. *mollachan*, a hillock	144
Millhàrry—G. *meall fhaire* (harry), watch-hill . .	143
Millifiàch—G. *meall a' fithiaich* (feeagh), raven's hill .	143
Millmòre—G. *meall mór*, great hill	143
Milmànnoch—G. *meall manach*, the monk's hill . .	143
Milnàb—G. *meall an aib*, the abbot's hill . . .	143
Mindòrk—G. *moine* (munny) *torc*, moor of the wild boars	123
Mòllanco ⎫ Mòlland ⎪ Mòllands ⎬ G. *mullán*, a hill	144
Mòllin ⎪	
Mùllion ⎭	
Mollandhù—G. *mullán dubh* (doo), black hill . .	144
Moncrìeff—G. *monadh craebh* (munny creav), moor of the trees	146

Index of Place-Names. 211

Monybùie—G. *monadh buidh* (munny buie), yellow moor . 146
Moniemòre—G. *monadh mór*, great moor . . . 146
Monygùile—G. *monadh goill*, the stranger's moor . . 146
Mòrar—G. *mór ard*, great height 15
Mòray—O.G. *mur mhagh* (vah, wah), sea-field . . 132
Mòrebattle—A.S. *mor botl*, moor-house . . . 62
Mòrrach—O.G. *mur mhagh* (vah, wah), sea-field . . 132
Mòrven—G. *mór bheinn* (ven), great hill . . . 15
Mounth, The—*monadh* (munny), a moorland . . 146
Mòuswald—N. *mosi völlr*, moss-field 89
Moy—O.G. *magh*, a plain or field 132
Muck (river)—G. (*amhuinn*) *muc*, sow's river . . 124
Mùckrach—G. *mucreach*, a swine pasture . . . 124
Mùiravonside—G. *mór amhuinn*, great stream (M.E. *side*, added) 9
Mùllach—G. *mullach*, a hill 144
Mullochàrd—G. *mullach ard*, high hill . . . 144
Mulwhàrker—G. *maol adhairce* (aharky), hill of the hunting-horn 119
Mùnnock—G. *monadh* (munny), a moor . . . 146
Mye—O.G. *magh*, a plain or field 132

Nairn (river)—G. (*amhuinn*) *na' fhearn* (ern), alder-river 46, 111
Nappers, The—N. *knappr*, hillocks 156
Nèsbustar } N. *nes bólstaðr*, house or farm at the cape . 92
Nìsabost }
Ness—G. *an eas* (ass), a cataract 172
Nèthan (river) — W. *afon eithin*, juniper or gorse river . 117
Nèwbattle—A.S. *niwe botl*, new house . . . 62
Nèwbigging—A.S. *niwe byggan*, new building . . 95

Ochteralìnachan—G. *uachdarach linachan*, upland of the flax-field 65, 118
Ochtralùre—G. *uachdarach lobhair* (lure), leper's upland 65, 170

Ochtrimakàin—G. *uachdarach mic Cain*, M'Kean's upland 65
Old Water—G. *allt*, a glen, a stream . . . 17, 18
Ord, The, of Caithness—G. *ard*, a height . . . 147
Òrkney—G. *orc*, N. *ey*, whale island 77
Ornòckenoch—G. *ard cnocnach*, height of the knolls . 147
Owen—G. *amhuinn* (avon, awn), a river . . . 9

Pàbay—N. *pap ey*, priest's isle 91
Palnèe—G. *pol an fhiaidh* (ee), the deer's stream . . 120
Palnùre—G. *pol n'iùbhar* (nure), water of the yews 37, 68, 113
Panbrìde—P. *lann Brighde*, St Bride's church . . 49
Panmùre—P. *lann mór*, great enclosure or church . . 49
Pàpa—N. *pap ey*, priest's isle 91
Pencòt—W. *pen coed*, wood-head 45
Penkìln—G. *pol cill*, the church stream . . . 46
Penmòlach—G. *peighinn molach*, rough or grassy penny-land 166
Pennyghàel—G. *peighinn Ghaeil*, the Gael's penny-land . 166
Pennygòwn—G. *peighinn gobhan* (gowan), the smith's penny-land 166
Petìllery—P. *pett iolaire* (yillary), eagle's croft . . 96
Piltànton—G. *pol shaint* (hant) *Antoin*, St Anthony's stream 176
Pitagòwan—P. *pett a' gobhain* (gowan), smith's croft . 62
Pitàrgus—P. *pett Fhearguis* (argus), Fergus's croft . 62
Pitcàirn—P. *pett carn*, mill-croft 64
Pitcàstle—P. *pett caiseail*, castle croft . . . 63
Pitèlpie—P. *pett Alpin*, Alpin's croft 179
Pitfòur—P. *pett fuar*, cold croft 62
Pitglàsso—P. *pett glasaich*, croft of green land . . 62
Pitgòwnie—P. *pett gamhnach* (gownah), milch-cows' croft 63
Pitkèerie—P. *pett caora*, sheep-croft 62
Pitlòchrie—P. *pett luacharach*, rushy croft . . . 117

Index of Place-Names. 213

Pitmèllan—P. *pett muileain* (meullan), mill-croft . . 64
Plàdda—N. *flatr ey*, flat isle 83
Port Leen—G. *puirt lín* (leen), flax port . . . 118
Portaclearys—G. *puirt a' clereich*, parson's port . . 177
Portàskaig—G. *puirt*, N. *askr vík*, landing-place of the ship's creek 90
Portbrìar—G. *puirt brathair* (brair), friar's port . . 177
Prèstwick—A.S. *preost wic*, priest's house . . . 90
Puldòuran—G. *pol doran*, otter burn 128
Pulfèrn—G. *pol fearn*, alder-water 10

Quìllichan—G. *coilleachan*, woodland . . . 107
Quils—G. *coill*, a wood 106
Quiràng—N. *kví rand*, round paddock . . . 88
Quoyschòrsetter—N. *kví schör setr*, paddock of the shore farm 87

Ràeden—A.S. *ra denn*, lair of the roe . . . 122
Ràehills—M.E. *rae hills*, roedeer hills . . . 122
Ràelees—M.E. *rae leas*, roedeer fields . . . 122
Raemòir ⎱
Raemòre ⎰ G. *reidh* (ray) *mór*, great flat . . 122, 165
Remòre ⎰
Rànna ⎱
Rànnoch ⎰ G. *raithneach* (rahnah), place of ferns . 115
Rànnas ⎰
Rànza ⎰
Rànnochan—G. *raithneachan* (rahnahan), place of ferns . 115
Rathèlpie—G. *rath Alpin*, Alpin's fort . . . 179
Reay—G. *reidh* (ray), flat land 165
Rebèg—G. *reidh beag*, little flat 165
Remòre—G. *reidh* (ray) *mór*, great flat . . . 165
Rephàd—G. *reidh* (ray) *fada*, long flat . . . 165
Ringdòo—G. *roinn dubh* (rinn doo), black point . . 166

214 Index of Place-Names.

Ringielàwn—G. *roinn na' leamhan* (rinn na lawn), elm-tree
    point 166
Ringùinea—G. *roinn Cinaeidh* (rinn kinna), Kenneth's
    portion 166
Risk ⎫
Rìskend ⎬ G. *riasg*, a marsh 163
Rìskhouse ⎭
Ròaldshay, North—N. *Rinan's ey*, Ringan's—*i.e.*, Ninian's
    isle 78, 173
Ròaldshay, South—N. *Rögnval's ey*, Ronald's isle . 78
Ròna ⎫
Rònay ⎬ N. *Rögn ey*, Ronan's isle 174
Rosnèath—G. *ros Nemhedh* (nevey), headland of Neved
                                               34, *note*
Ròxburgh—A.S. *Rauic's burh*, Rawic's town . . 14
Rum—O.G. (*i*) *dhruim* (hruim), ridge-island . . 85
Rùsco ⎫
Rùskich ⎬ G. *riasgach*, marshy land 163
Rùskie ⎭
Ruthwell (pron. Rìvvel)—A.S. *róde well*, rood or cross
    well 39

St Enoch's—M.E. *St Thenew's or Theneuke's*, mother of
    St Kentigern 175
Sàlachan—G. *saileachean*, the willows . . . 112
Sàlachry—G. *saileachreach*, a place of willows . . 112
Sanaigmòre—N. *sand vík*, G. *mór*, great sandy bay . 84
Sànnox—N. *sand vík*, sandy bay 86
Sànquhar (pron. Sànker)—G. *sean cathair* (shan caher),
    old fort 14
Sàuchie—A.S. *sealh*, the willow 112
Sàuchrie—G. *saileachreach*, a place of willows . . 112
Scràbba ⎫
Scràbbie ⎬ G. *scrath* (scraw) *bo*, cow sward or pasture . 125

Index of Place-Names. 215

Scrapehàrd } Scraphàrd } G. *scrath* (scraw) *ard*, high sward . .	165
Sèaforth—N. *sœ fjörðr*, sea firth	84
Sèlkirk—N. *skáli kirkju*, the shieling kirk . . .	102
Sènwick—N. *sand vík*, sandy bay	86
Sgurr a' bhealaich dheirg (a vallich harrig)—G. hill of the red pass	152
Sgurr a' choire ghlas (a horry hlass)—G. hill of the green corry	152
Sgurr na choinich (hōnigh)—G. hill of the gathering, assembly hill	151
Shàlloch—G. *sealg* (shallug), the chase . . .	119
Shàmbelly } Shànballie } G. *sean baile* (shan bally), old place . .	14
Shànavalley Shànavallie Shànvalley Shànvolley } G. *sean bhaile* (shan valley), old place Shènval Shènvalla Shìnvollie	14, 134
Shèshader—N. *sœ setr*, sea shieling	93
Sìnniness—N. *sunnr nes*, south point . . .	86, 89
Skaith } Skate } G. *sgitheach* (skeaghe), hawthorn . . .	113
Skeòch } Skeòg } G. *sgitheog* (skeog), hawthorn . . .	113
Slaehàrbrie—G. *sliabh Chairbre* (slew harbrie), Cairbre's moor	141
Slamànnan—G. *sliabh* (slieve or slew) *Manann*, moor of the Picts of Manann	39, 141
Slate Islands—E. producing roofing-slate . . .	141
Slayhòrrie—G. *sliabh choire* (slew horry), moor of the corry	141

216   *Index of Place-Names.*

Sleat—G. *sleibhte* (slatey), the hills 141
Slewcàirn—G. *sliabh carn*, moor of the cairns . . 141
Slewnàrk—G. *sliabh n' adhairce* (slew naharky), moor of
    the hunting-horn 120
Slewsmìrroch—G. *sliabh* (slieve, slew) *smeurach*, black-
    berry moor 114, 141
Sliagh—G. *sliabh* (slew), a moor 141
Sligh—? G. *sliabh* (slew), a moor 141
Slouchnagàrie—G. *slochd na' caora*, sheep's gulley . 82
Smirle—G. *smeurlach* (smerrlah), a place of blackberries . 114
Smòorage—G. *smeurach*, a place of blackberries . . 114
Snìzort (pron. Sneezort)—N. *Sneis fjörðr*, Sney's firth 84, 90
Stab Hill—O.G. *stob*, a peak 152
Stac-meall-na-cuaich—G. hill-peak of the cuckoo . . 152
Stàffa—N. *stafa ey*, staff-island 91
Stànhope—N. *stein hóp*, stone shelter or glen . . 89
Stènnis—N. *stein nes*, cape of the (standing) stones . 89
Stob ban—G. white peak 152
Stob choire an easain mhor (horrie an assanvore)—G. peak
    of the corry of the great waterfall . . . 152
Stòneykirk—A.S. *Steeny circ*, Stephen's kirk . . 74
Stòrnoway—N. *Stjarna vágr*, Stjarna's bay . . . 90
Strath Òssian—O.G. *srath oisin* (oshin), strath of the red-
    deer calves 121
Strathbùngo—G. *srath Mungo*, strath of the gracious one
    —*i.e.*, St Kentigern 175
Strathèarn—? G. *srath Erann*, the vale of the Ernai . 36
Strathỳre—G. *srath fheoir* (ire), grassy strath . . 116
Stroan }
Strone } G. *sron*, the nose, a point 48
Stronachlàcher—G. *sron a' chlachair*, the mason's point 48, 169
Stròwan }
Strùan } G. *sruthan* (sruhan), the streams . . 48
Stuck—G. *stuc*, a peak 152

Index of Place-Names. 217

Stuckentàggart—G. *stuc an t-shagairt* (taggart), the priest's peak 152
Stuckievièwlich—G. *stuc a' bhualaich* (vewaligh), peak of the cattle-fold 152
Swarehead—A.S. *sweora*, the neck 102
Swìndridge—M.E. swine ridge 123
Swìnhill—M.E. swine hill 123
Swìnton—M.E. *swine tún*, enclosure of the swine . . 123
Swire—A.S. *sweora*, the neck ; L. *jugum* . . . 102
Swòrdale—N. *svarðar dalr*, dale of the greensward 88, 89
Sẏmington—O.N.E. *Simon tún*, Simon's town . . 101

Tàbost—N. *hallr bólstaðr*, sloping farm . . . 83
Tandragèe—G. *ton le gaeith* (geuh, gwee), backside to the wind 162
Tànnach ⎫
Tànnoch ⎬ G. *tamhnach* (tawnah), a meadow . . 165
Tànnock ⎭
Tannyflùx—G. *tamhnach fliuch*, wet meadow . . 165
Tannyròach—G. *tamhnach ruadh* (tawnah rooah), red meadow 165
Tàrbet—G. *tarruin bád*, draw-boat 71
Tarbrèoch—? O.G. *tír bréach*, wolf-land . . . 127
Tardòw—G. *tír dubh* (doo), black land . . . 131
Tarf ⎫ (rivers)—G. (*amhuinn*) *tarbh* (tarriv), river of the
Tarth ⎭ bulls 124
Tarwìlkie—G. *treabh* (trav) *giolcach*, broom-farm . . 131
Teràlly—G. *tír Amhalghaidh* (Owlhay), Olaf's or Aulay's land 82
Terrègles—G. *treamhar* (traver) *eglais*, church land . 131
Thamnabhaidh (Hàmnavoe)—N. *höfn vágr*, haven bay . 84
Thànkerton—O.N.E. *Thancard tún*, Thancard's house . 101
Thìrlestane—A.S. *þirle stœn*, bored stone . . . 123
Tìbbers—G. *tiobar*, a well 176

218   Index of Place-Names.

Tìngwall—N. *þinga völlr*, the assembly field	89
Tinlùskie—G. *tír loisgthe* (luskie), burnt land	131
Tìnwald—N. *þinga völlr*, the assembly field	89
Tiràrgus—G. *tír Fhearguis* (ergus), Fergus's land	131
Tiree—G. *tír idhe* (ee), corn-land	11, 131
Tirfèrgus—G. *tír Fearguis*, Fergus's land	131
Tobermòry—G. *tiobar Muire*, Mary's well	172
Tòdhope—N. *tod hóp*, fox-shelter	101
Tòdley—O.N.E. *tod lea*, fox-field	135
Toldòw—G. *tol dubh* (doo), black hole	164
Tòllo ⎫ Tòlly ⎭ G. *tulach*, a hill	151
Tolrònald—G. *tol Raonuill*, Ronald's hole	164
Tonderghìe (pron. Tondergèe)—G. *ton le gaeith* (geuh, gwee), backside to the wind	162
Tòrmisdale—N. *Orm's dalr*, Orm's dale	83
Tòrran ⎫ Tòrrance ⎬ G. *torran*, the hillocks, or *torrán*, a hillock Tòrrans ⎭	156
Torrs, The—G. *torr*, a round steep hill	156
Tòrwoodlee—G. *torr*, a round steep hill, M.E. *wode lea*, the field of the hill wood	156
Tràmmond Ford—G. *troman*, elder-bush	112
Troon—W. *trwyn*, the nose, a point	49
Tròtternish ⎫ Trùddernish ⎭ N. *trylldir nes*, enchanted cape	89
Tròwgrain—N. *trog grein*, trough branch (of a stream)	101
Truim (river)—G. (*amhuinn*) *truim*, elder-bush river	112
Tùllich ⎫ Tùllo ⎬ G. *tulach*, a hill Tùlloch ⎭	151
Uist—G. *i-fheirste* (eehurst), ford-island	85
Ùlbster—N. *Ulfr bólstaðr*, Ulf's farm	127

Index of Place-Names.

Ullapool—N. *Olafr bólstaðr*, Olaf's farm . . . 82
Ulsta—N. *Ulfr bólstaðr*, Ulf's farm 127
Ulva—N. *ulfa ey*, wolf-island 91
Ure (river)—G. (*amhuinn*) *iubhar* (yure), river of the yews 37
Urie (river)—G. (*amhuinn*) *iubheraich* (yūreh), river of the yew-wood 37, 113

Whithorn—A.S. *hwit œrn*, white house . . . 3
Wick—N. *vík*, the bay or creek 90
Windhouse—N. *vind áss*, windy ridge . . . 84
Wolfstar—N. *Ulfr bólstaðr*, Ulf's farm . . 92, 127
Wrath, Cape—N. *hvarf*, a turning-point . . . 23

Yarrow—G. (*amhuinn*) *garbh* (garriv), rough stream 138, 171
Yearn Gill—N. *örn gil*, eagle's ravine . . . 97
Yester—? W. *ystrad*, the strath or vale . . 49
York—G. *Eburach*, the place of Ebor or Eburus . 140

www.ingramcontent.com/pod-product-compliance
Lightning Source LLC
Chambersburg PA
CBHW050143170426
43197CB00011B/1941